30

인도네시아 판례

INDONESIA

DOMESTIC & INTERNATIONAL CASES

Jihyun Park | Galih D. Ramadhan | Yulio Iqbal C.A | Alif M. Gultom

YONSEI UNIVERSITY PRESS

이 저서는 2020년도 정부(교육과학기술부)의 재원으로 한국연구재단의 지원을 받아 수행된 해외 공동연구지원사업임.(NRF-2020S1A5A2A03040483)

30

인도네시아 판례

INDONESIA

DOMESTIC & INTERNATIONAL CASES

Jihyun Park | Galih D. Ramadhan | Yulio Iqbal C.A | Alif M. Gultom

YONSEI UNIVERSITY PRESS

Contents

Author

Jihyun Park

1. Ligitan & Sipadan Island
2. DS484 Halal
3. DS406 Clove Cigarettes
3. DS467 Tobacco Plain Packaging
5. ASEAN Charter-Constitution Court
6. Shiseido Traditional Knowledge
7. Ache LGBT Couple
8. MPL Forest Fire

Yulio Iqbal Cahyo Arsetyo

1. East Timor
2. Rawagede 1948
3. Massacare 1965
4. Aceh Conflict 1979
5. Indonesia Reformation 1998
6. Mc. Donald House Bombing
7. Sinking Illegal Fishing Vessels in Indonesia
8. DS496 Galvalum

Galih D. Ramadhan

1. Toyota Motor Corp. v. io Teddy Siswanto
2. DC Comics, Inc. v. PT. Marxing Fam Makmur
3. HUGO BOSS v. Teddy Tan & Alexander
4. Inter IKEA System B.V. v. PT. Ratania Khatulistiwa
5. John Hardy Jewelry & PT. Karya Tangan Indah v. Ketut Deni Aryasa
6. Indonesia Monkey Selfie Picture
7. Death Sentence for International Drug Traffickers
8. Sampit Conflict 2001
9. Bali Bombing 2002

Alif Muhammad Gultom

1. DS312 Certain Paper
2. DS480 Biodisel
3. Churchill Mining PLC
4. Rafat Ali Rizvi v. Indonesia
5. Chandra and others v. Netherlands

Abbreviation

Additional Protocol I (AP I)	Protocol additional to the Geneva Conventions of 12 August 1949, and relating to the Protection of Victims of International Armed Conflicts (Protocol I), 8 June 1977
Additional Protocol II (AP II)	Protocol additional to the Geneva Conventions of 12 August 1949, and relating to the Protection of Victims of Non-International Armed Conflicts (Protocol II), 8 June 1977
Additional Protocol III (AP III)	Protocol additional to the Geneva Conventions of 12 August 1949, and relating to the Adoption of an Additional Distinctive Emblem (Protocol III), 8 December 2005
1977 Additional Protocols	Additional Protocols I and II
Amended Protocol II to the Convention on Certain Conventional Weapons	Protocol II to the Convention on Certain Conventional Weapons of 10 October 1980 (Amended Protocol II), as amended on 3 May 1996
ASEAN	Association of Southeast Asian Nations (Indonesia, Thailand, Malaysia, Singapore, Philippines, Vietnam, Brunei, Cambodia, Myanmar'Burma', Lao DPR)
ASEAN Charter	Constituent instrument of the ASEAN
Berne Convention	Convention for the Protection of Literary and Artistic Works
BKPM	(in Bahasa: Badan Koordinasi Penanaman Modal) Indonesian Investment Coordinating Board is a Non-Ministerial Government Agency, which in charge of implementing policy and service coordination in investment in accordance with the provisions of the regulations

CIHL	Customary International Humanitarian Law
Common Article 1	Article 1 common to the Geneva Conventions of 12 August 1949
Common Article 2	Article 2 common to the Geneva Conventions of 12 August 1949
Common Article 3	Article 3 common to the Geneva Conventions of 12 August 1949
Convention against Torture	Convention against Torture and Other Cruel, Inhuman or Degrading Treatment or Punishment, 10 December 1984
DJKI	(in Bahasa: Direktorat Jendral Kekayaan Intelektual) Directorate General of Intellectual Property, an Echelon I organizational unit under Indonesia Ministry of Law and Human Rights of the Republic of Indonesia, which is tasked with implementing IPR protection management and services in Indonesia, for Patents, Trademarks, Copyrights, Industrial Designs, Layout Designs of Integrated Circuits, Trade Secrets, and Geographical Indications .
EC	European Community
ECHR	European Court of Human Rights
EEZ	Exclusive Economic Zone
EU	European Union
1949 Geneva Conventions (GC I, II, III and IV)	Convention (I) for the Amelioration of the Condition of the Wounded and Sick in Armed Forces in the Field, 12 August 1949 (First Geneva Convention) Convention (II) for the Amelioration of the Condition of Wounded, Sick and Shipwrecked Members of Armed Forces at Sea, 12 August 1949 (Second Geneva Convention)

	Convention (III) relative to the Treatment of Prisoners of War, 12 August 1949 (Third Geneva Convention) Convention (IV) relative to the Protection of Civilian Persons in Time of War, 12 August 1949 (Fourt Geneva Convention)
1994 GATT	The General Agreement on Tariffs and Trade
Hague Convention No. V	Convention No. V respecting the Rights and Duties of Neutral Powers and Persons in Case of War on Land, The Hague, 18 October 1907
Hague Convention No. XIII	Convention No. XIII concerning the Rights and Duties of Neutral Powers in Naval War, The Hague, 18 October 1907
Hague Regulations	Convention No. IV respecting the Laws and Customs of War on Land and its annex: Regulations concerning the Laws and Customs of War on Land, The Hague, 18 October 1907
ICC	International Criminal Court
ICCPR	International Covenant on Civil and Political Rights
ICJ	International Court of Justice
ICJ Statue	Statute of the International Court of Justice annexed to the Charter of the United Nations, 26 June 1945
ICRC	International Committee of the Red Cross
ICSID	International Center for Settlement of Investment Dispute
ICTY	International Criminal Tribunal for the former Yugoslavia
ICTR	International Criminal Tribunal for Rwanda

IHL	International Humanitarian Law
ILC	International Law Commission
IPT	International People Tribunal 1965
NGO	Non-Governmental Organisation
PCIJ	Permanent Court of International Justice
1998 Rome statute	A Treaty that established the International Criminal Court (ICC)
SC Res.	United Nations Security Council
S.Ct	US Supreme Court, Supreme Court Reporter
TRIPs	The Agreement on Trade-Related Aspects of Intellectual Property Rights
UNCLOS	United Nations Convention for the Law of the Sea
UNTS	United Nations Treaty Series
UN Doc	United Nations Document
U.S.	US Supreme Court, United States Reports
USC	United States Code
Rome Statute	Rome Statute of the International Criminal Court, 17 July 1998
UN	United Nations
UN Charter	Charter of the United Nations, San Francisco, 26 June 1945
Vienna Convention	An international agreement regulating treaties between states
WIPO	World Intellectual Property Organization

Latin

ad hoc	For this purpose (only)
aanslag	Separatism, the attempt undertaken with the intent to bring the territory of the state wholly or partially under foreign domination or to separate part
cide	An act of killing
de facto	Existing as a matter of fact
de jure	Existing as a matter of law
effectiviès	Effective, "colonial effectivitès" referring to the conduct of the administrative authorities as proof of the effective exercise of territorial jurisdiction in the region during the colonial period
erga omnes	Opposable to, valid against, 'all the world', i.e. all other legal persons irrespective of consent on the part of those thus affected.
exceptio obscuur libel	The lawsuit is vague and unclear
exceptio plurium litis consortium	Lawsuit Error in persona in the form of fewer parties
force majeure	Under the influence of duress
fortiori	Adv. By the stronger; with better reason; all the more
genos	People or race
horse de combat	(a) anyone who is in the power of an adverse party; (b) anyone who is defenceless because of unconsciousness, shipwreck, wounds or sickness; or (c) anyone who clearly expresses an intention to surrender; provided he or she abstains from any hostile act and does not attempt to escape
ipso facto	That very fact or act

jus ad bellum	Refers to the right to make war
jus cogens	Preemptory norms of general international law
jus in bello	Related to the laws and customs of war
les effets de la guerre	Effects of the outbreak of war
opinio juris	A subjective obligation, a sense on behalf of a state that it is bound to the law in question. In customary international law, element necessary to establish a legally binding custom
per se	By itself
pacta sunt servanda	Simply, the principle that agreement are binding and are to be implemented in good faith
premature	The lawsuit is too early
prima facie	In principle; presumptively
quid pro quo	Something given or received for something else
state decisis	[to stand by things decided] A maxim expressing the underlying basis of the doctrine of "precedent". The decision of that ICJ have no binding force except between the parties and in respect of that particular case
sui generis	Of its own kind. Unique. Not falling within the normal legal categories
travaux prèparatories	Preparatory work; preliminary drafts, minutes of conferences, and the like, relating to the conclusion of a treaty
utile non devet per inutile vitiari	That which is useful or valid ought not to be vitiated by that which is suprefluous or invalid
ultra vires	Beyond authority; in excess of authority
uti posidentis	One of the praetorian interdicts under the civil law, deriving its name from the introductory words of the formula appropriate to it
utile non devet per inutile vitiari	Useful or valid ought not to be vitiated by that which is superfluous or invalid

Preface

In 2020, I and prof.dodik have applied for a Joint Research Project covering the topic of "Data Law and Policy on Immigration Control" and our topic was selected by the National Research Foundation of Korea. This book is the first publication after we started this research. I have suggested Indonesian case book because first, this research covers Korea and Indonesia and second, there is not many of the book introducing Indonesian laws and policies in Korea. To understand Indonesian laws and policies, together with Indonesian students participating in a dual degree (graduate, undergraduate) course, the authors have selected and analyzed 30 cases considering importance in Indonesian society.

We have tried to deliver facts and precedents as objectively and faithfully as possible. key arguments to be conveyed in precedents or content that the authors want to add to this precedent are added in the comments. Authors also have provided a key point to remember in each case. 'key principle' in case of formal trials, and 'key point' in case of other forms of the trial has been designated.

It took over a year to write the book. Each person selected the case of interest and prepared a draft, and Galih finished the indexing. I like to express great gratitude to co-author students. All three of them are proud students of the first law school in Indonesia, the Universe Islam Indonesia (UII), and I wish them the best. The three students were also students of Prof. Jawahir Thontowi, Prof. Agus Triyanta, Prof. Dodik Setiawan Nur Heriyanto, Prof. Budi Agus Riswandi of UII. Advice and insight from them on the cases added great value to the book. I like to thank them for helping us to introduce the Indonesian case book in Korea.

I am grateful to Prof. Dae-soon Kim for his academic integrity and inspiration, and Prof. Jeong-Oh Kim for teaching me an attractive philosophy of law. Dr. Eun-beom Choi of the Korean Red Cross, who taught me an international humanitarian law, is currently struggling with the disease, and I wish him a speedy recovery.

Most of all, I thank my beloved husband Sung-Joo Park who keeps me balanced spiritually in this life and my daughter Mira who shows me the 1000 lux smile. Thank you to the president of Yonsei University Press for accepting the publication of this book.

- Jihyun park

Indonesia is a country with rich culture and natural resources. The 4th of the most populous country in the world with an amazing workforce. With all these resources, Indonesia surely can become the next superpower with the vision of Indonesia Golden 2045.

I had many experiences before this book especially under the supervision of Professor Jawahir Thontowi, of UII's supervision, but this time this is a little bit different. This time, it is not just assisting but writing the book. This is the first time I write the book as the author rather than credited as the assistant researcher.

I would like to give my gratitude to my Parents, My Little Brother, Professor Jawahir Thontowi, CLDS, Universitas Islam Indonesia, and Youngsan University, Prof. Jihyun Park and all the amazing Professors that I found there. Without them, this will not happen.

In this book, I had written many cases linked with some of Indonesia's past human rights. I believe that the stability of investment from western countries always linked with the human rights factor in a nation. It becomes crucial to show the world how we Indonesia can resolve our past human right issue and march forward to the Golden Age of Indonesia in 2045. The past human rights issue always become "haunting ghosts" that haunted the nation every special moment in Indonesia that shackle Indonesia to going forward.

We can learn this from the Republic of Korea, one of the biggest trading partners of Indonesia. Where they did not deny and accepted their past after the Gwangju Uprising in 1980. The Republic of Korea concluded that the story of oppression and opened a new chapter of democracy using as a growth engine making Republic Korea as we know it today. My writing is no means to discredit my beloved Country. This is just a friendly reminder and an assessment of what we Indonesian can archive when we conclude the past by following the precedent of the Republic of Korea, our Friends.

- Yulio Iqbal Cahyo Arsetyo on behalf of the three Indonesian co-researchers

Acknowledgement

Legal Scholar Views Related to the Indonesian Legal System and Human Rights: A Legal Scholar's Genuine Review of the Implementation of Law and Human Rights Based on Facts and Cases of Indonesian and International Courts

By
Jawahir Thontowi
Professor of Legal Anthropology Universitas Islam Indonesia

This book gives some intriguing insights into how the international community views Indonesia particularly concerning the legal cases that are resolved by the state. The book covers a wide range of interesting and important cases which had put Indonesia under international scrutiny particularly concerning issues of human rights, state territory, international relations, business, and the environment. Furthermore, the books provide an analysis of how the Indonesian government during different presidential terms has managed international disputes with other countries using a range of methods from a peace-based approach and a military-based approach.

The issues covered in this book are quite controversial in Indonesia and this cannot be separated from the efforts of an academician to seek answers which certainly invites appreciation but also warrants some critical thoughts. One such aspect is the approach that the book takes. Although the book provides an elaborate and impressive case by case analysis, however, unfortunately, the pros and cons of views and opinions of the Indonesian people can not be represented fully in this book. This is important to note that the patterns of law in Indonesia are not only constrained by the legal context of the courts or international agreements but also the norms and customs, valid in Indonesian society. It is certainly plausible to use Law and International Agreements as a benchmark for evaluating specific cases in Indonesia, however, such analysis would be enriched when it includes the aspects of norms and customs valid in Indonesia. I believe that this was possible since 3 of the authors are Indonesian citizens who would have access to sources and facts concerning the sociological conditions of Indonesia which would be able to give a more balanced perspective of the issue.

Despite this, the book entitled "*30 Indonesia Domestic & International Cases*" is not merely an impressive academic endeavor, but it also provides new insights concerning the Indonesian state's response toward international public law and human rights. In elaborating her argument, she highlights the relevance of Indonesia's history as related to the legal foundations of Indonesian society. Accordingly, in 1200 AD, Islam entered Indonesia and Islam continued to have a sustaining influence on Indonesia's past and contemporary legal system. In contrast to the current approach Indonesian legal scholars use to analyze national cases, Prof. Jihyun Park provides a novel analysis by applying a common law approach toward Indonesian legal cases. From the Legal perspective, prof. Jihyun Park's work is important since it introduces Indonesian law and law enforcement by exploring and analyzing facts and cases within the Indonesian context by applying a pure theory of positivism of International law, obligations, consisting of an international convention or Jus *Cogen*, or the *Erga Omnes*, obligation to examine the case of Aceh belligerency and East Timor's separation from Indonesia which led it to become an independent state. In the modern Indonesia context, Indonesia has made a significant contribution to regional politics for example involvement in the ASEAN organization. In practice, however, in order to achieve greater international standing, Indonesia as a country, a government together with its legal enforcing role, should not be involved in any form of human rights violation.

It is very rare to find a foreign legal scholar who writes on Indonesian issues and also discusses political situations in Indonesia. Therefore, I believe that Prof. Jihyun Park and her students have explored and analyzed facts and cases of Indonesia which would enrich knowledge by employing a creative and critical yet constructive approach. I appreciate the fact that Prof. Jihyun Park and her students endeavored to publish the book in both English and Indonesian considering the relevance in both national and international contexts.

Brief History of Indonesia

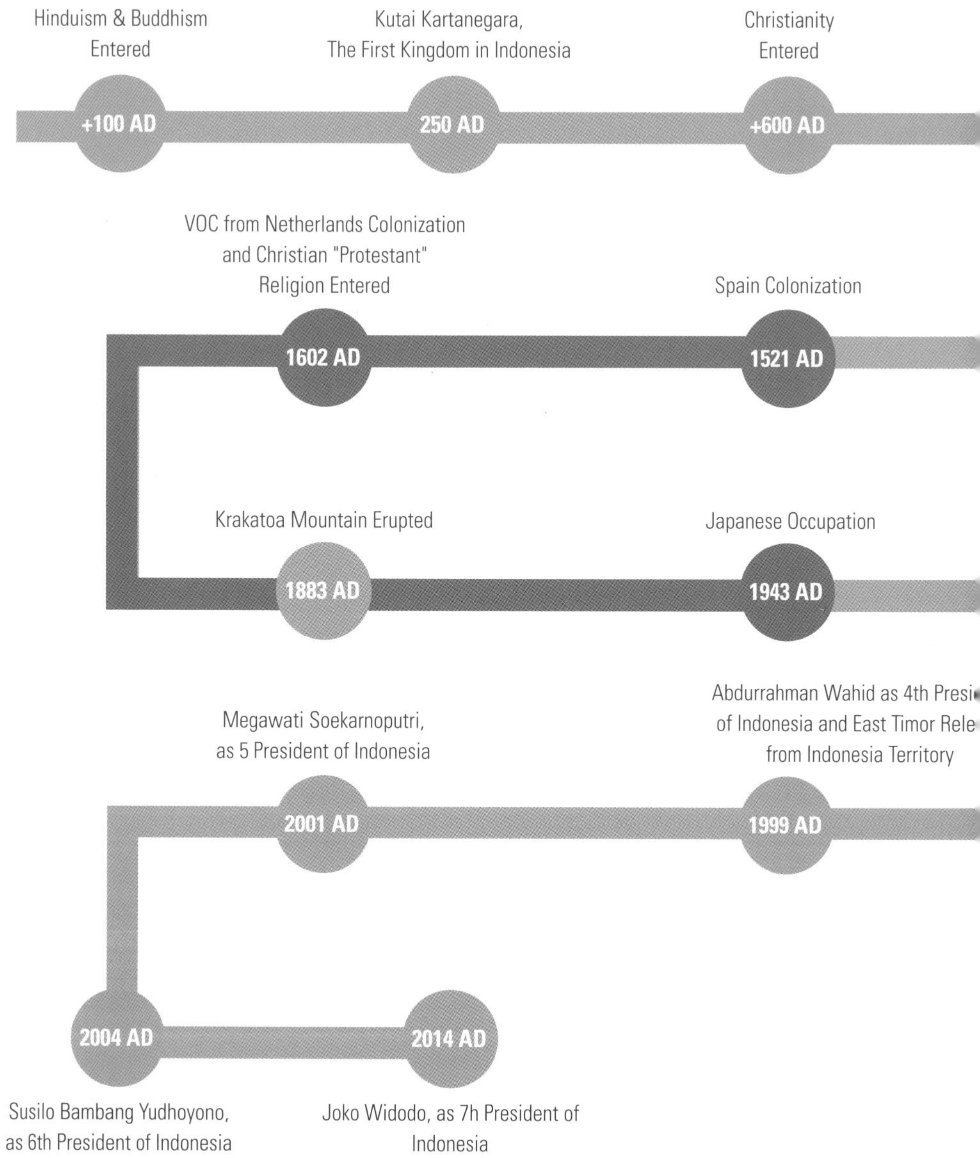

682 AD — Sriwijaya, Large Maritime Kingdom in Indonesia

824 AD — Candi Borobudur, The Largest Buddhist Temple in The World was built

856 AD — Candi Prambanan, One of the largest Hindu Temple in Southeast Asia was constructed

+1200 AD — Islam Entered

1350 AD — Majapahit Kingdom Ruled Across Nusantara

1509 AD — Portuguese Colonization and Christian "Catholic" Religion entered

1945 AD — Indonesia Independence, Soekarno as 1" President of Indonesia

1950 AD — Indonesia join United Nation & GATT

1967 AD — Soeharto as 2nd President of Indonesia. ASEAN was Established

1995 AD — Indonesia become Member of World Trade Organization

1998 AD — Indonesia Reformation, Bacharuddin Jusuf Habibie as 3rd President of Indonesia

Part I

Territory Cases

1. Sipadan & Ligitan Island Case

2. East Timor Case

3. Sinking Illegal Fishing Vessels in Indonesia

I Territory Cases

1. Ligitan & Sipadan Island Case[1]

Key Principle: In the case of a very small island which is uninhabited that has little economic importance (at least until recently) where the legal title is not capable of showing exactly the territorial expanse to which it relates, the *Effectivitès* can play an essential role in showing how the title is interpreted in practice

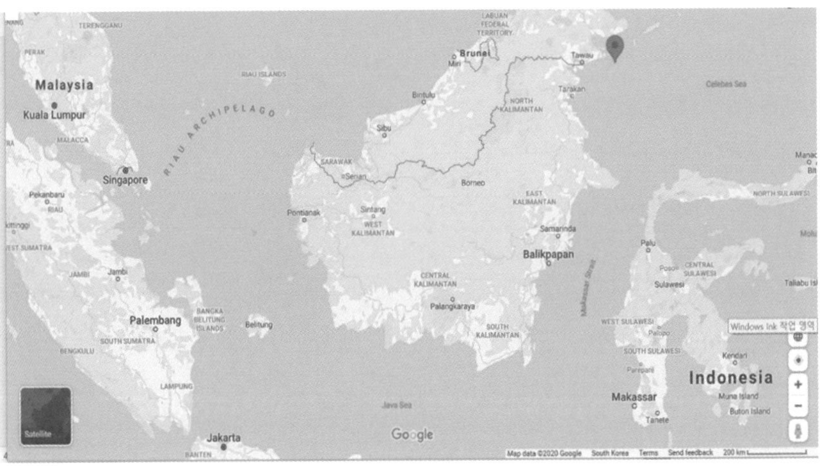

1) Facts

In 1969, Indonesia and Malaysia were negotiating the continental shelf[2].

---

1) Case concerning soverignty over pulau ligitan and pulau sipadan (Indoneisa v. Malaysia), Judgement of 23 October 2001, ICJ Report 2001.

2) For the definition of the continental shelf, please refer 1. presidential proclamation No. 2267 concerning the Policy of the United States with respect to the Natural Resources of the Subsoil and Seabed of the Continental Shelf 2. 1958 Geneva Convention on the Continental Shelf 3. UN Convention on the Law of the Sea. For related cases, 1. Anglo-Norwegian Fisheries Case(the United Kingdom v. Norway) ICJ Reports (1951) 2. North Sea Continental Shelf Case (Federal Republic of Germany/Denmark) ICJ Reports 1969 3. Continental Shelf (Tunisia/Libya) ICJ Reports 1982 4. Maritime Delimitation and Territorial Questions between Qatar and Bahrain (Qatar/Bahrain) ICJ Judgment of 16 March 2001 5. Delamination of the Maritime Boundary

UN Charter Art. 2(3), Art. 33(1) ask settling disputes in peaceful means and UNCLOS Art. 278(1) obligates states to settle disputes by peaceful means. These are the international materials pushing countries to negotiate maritime boundaries[3]. When Indonesia discovered that Malaysia is building facilities on Pulau Sipadan, dispute intensified in 1991. Both Indonesia and Malaysia claimed sovereignty over the Ligitan and Sipadan Islands[4]. Indonesia claimed sovereignty with three grounds[5]. First, Convention which Great Britain and the Netherlands agreed in 1891 Second, as the successor to the Sultan of Bulungan. Third, *effectivitès*. Malaysia claimed on the two grounds. The series of alleged transmission of the title originally held by the former sovereign, the Sultan of Sulu and *effectivitès*.

2) Court Decision

First, Indonesia based the claim that the establishment of 4°10' N parallel of latitude considering the objective and purpose of the 1891 Convention[6] and the terms written in 1891 Convention purposed the Parties' respective possession of the land relying on the Article IV of the 1891 Convention[7].

---

between Bangladesh and Myanmar in the by of Bengal case, ITLOS Judgment of 14 March 2012 6. Territorial and Maritime Disputes (Nicaragua v. Columbia), ICJ Judgement of 19 November 2012.

3) Eddy Pratomo, "Negotiation on Maritime Delimination: Indonesian Practice", Proceedings of the 5th Joint International Conference of Youngsan University, Busan, Korea, 2019.

4) Both islands are in the Celebes Sea, off the north-east coast of the island of Borneo, and lie approximately 15.5 nautical miles apart. Ligitan island stays above sea level. It is made of sand covered with low-lying vegetation and some trees. It is not permanently inhabited. Sipadan is a densely wooded island of volcanic origin and the top of a submarine mountain some 600 to 700 in height. It was not inhabited permanently until the 1980s later developed as a tourist resort. ICJ report of judgments, para 14.

5) Indonesia has more than 17,000 islands and 10 neighboring countries.

6) Although Indonesia is not a party to the Vienna Convention of 23 May 1969 on the Law of Treaties, customary international law is recognized and applied.

7) "From 4°10' North latitude on the east coast the boundary-line shall be continued eastward along that parallel, across the Island of Sebatik: that portion of the island situated to the north of that parallel shall belong unreservedly to the British North Borneo Company and the portion south of that parallel to the Netherlands".

Two parties submitted different interpretation on the "boundary-line shall be continued" and "across" providing disagreement on the term[8]. The Court therefore referred to the Dutch Explanatory Memorandum appended to the draft Law submitted to the Netherlands State-General which includes prior negotiation agreement and map concluding these documents concluding these cannot be the evidence of agreement relating to the conclusion of the treaty[9] in Art 31 of the Vienna Convention.[10] Instead, the 1891 Convention intended the delimitation of Netherlands possession in the island of Borneo and States in that island[11]. While looking into the evidence, the Court also examined the *travaux prèparatories* and subsequent conduct of the parties.

Second, the Court looked into the claim of title by succession[12]. Indonesia claimed that the original titleholder, Sultan of Bulungan gave a

---

8) Paras. 39-43.

9) Paras. 44-48.

10) Article 31 General rule of interpretation

1. A treaty shall be interpreted in good faith in accordance with the ordinary meaning to be given to the terms of the treaty in their context and in the light of its object and purpose.
2. The context for the purpose of the interpretation of a treaty shall comprise, in addition to the text, including its preamble and annexes:
   (a) any agreement relating to the treaty which was made between all the parties in connexion with the conclusion of the treaty; (b) any instrument which was made by one or more parties in connexion with the conclusion of the treaty and accepted by the other parties as an instrument related to the treaty.
3. There shall be taken into account, together with the context:
   (a) any subsequent agreement between the parties regarding the interpretation of the treaty or the application of its provisions; (b) any subsequent practice in the application of the treaty which establishes the agreement of the parties regarding its interpretation; (c) any relevant rules of international law applicable in the relations between the parties.
4. A special meaning shall be given to a term if it is established that the parties so intended.
   Article 32 Supplementary means of interpretation
   Recourse may be had to supplementary means of interpretation, including the preparatory work of the treaty and the circumstances of its conclusion, in order to confirm the meaning resulting from the application of article 31, or to determine the meaning when the interpretation according to article 31:
   (a) leaves the meaning ambiguous or obscure; or (b) leads to a result which is manifestly absurd or unreasonable.

11) Paras. 49-51.

12) Paras. 93-125.

title to the Netherlands then to Indonesia.

Malaysia also contended that it has transferred ownership from the original holder the Sultan of Sulu. Malaysia's historical transfer of the title has started from Sultan of Sulu to Spain to the United States, Britain on behalf of the State of North Borneo, the United Kingdom of Great Britain and Northern Ireland and Malaysia as a last source of the sovereign.

Denying the contention of both countries, the Court looked into the evidence of effective sovereign authority provided by both countries as a last resort. Indonesia cited patrols in the area by vessels of the Dutch Royal Navy, activities of the Indonesian Navy in addition to the traditional use by Indonesian fishermen. Malaysia cited the Turtle Preservation Ordinance of 1917 which lasted effectively until the 1950s at least and was applied in the area of two disputed islands. This ordinance was enacted and enforced by the North Borneo authority. 1962 construction of a lighthouse on Sipadan and 1963 construction of a lighthouse on Ligitan by the authority of the colony of North Borneo continued its operation by Malaysia since its independence. The Court foundout that the Indonesian government never raised any objection at that time or after.

Comparing administrative actions taken by both countries, ICJ separated the act of private persons characterizing the act of fishermen who are private persons cannot be seen as *effectivitès* if they do not take place on the basis of official regulations or under governmental authority. In contrast, actions taken by Malaysia were legislative, administrative, and quasi-judicial activities that were diverse in character therefore ICJ considered it to be a pattern of intention and act of sovereign. ICJ by citing below concluded that the sovereignty over Palau Ligitan and Pulau Sipadan belongs to Malaysia on the basis of the *effectivitès*.

> "134. The Court first recalls the statement by the Permanent Court of International Justice in the Legal Status of Eastern Greenland (Denmark v. Norway) case: "a claim to sovereignty based not upon some particular act or title such as a treaty of cession but merely

upon continued display of authority involves two elements each of which must be shown to exist: the intention and will to act as sovereign, and some actual exercise or display of such authority."

The Permanent Court continued:

"It is impossible to read the records of the decisions in cases as to territorial sovereignty without observing that in many cases the tribunal has been satisfied with very little in the way of the actual exercise of sovereign rights, provided that the other State could not make out a superior claim. This is particularly true in the case of claims to sovereignty over areas in thinly populated or unsettled countries." (P.C.I. J., Series AIB, No. 53, pp. 45-46.)

In particular, in the case of very small islands which are uninhabited or not permanently inhabited - like Ligitan and Sipadan, which have been of little economic importance (at least until recently) - *effectivitès* will indeed generally be scarce.

3) Comments

(1) *Effectivitès*

Is a geographical element a piece of decisive evidence that can be the condition to the legal sovereignty in territorial disputes? Geographical element has been used to decide the baseline of the maritime frontiers. However, it has not been the decisive evidence over a legal title or effective control. In the case of Minquiers and ecrehos[13)], the island group title has been given to the United Kingdom when the geographical location is much closer to France. Also, the title of the Pedra Branca Island that is closer to Malaysia geographically end up to Singapore due to the conduct as the

13) (France vs. UK), ICJ Reports (1953), p.47.

operator of Horsburgh lighthouse, investigation of marine accidents, their control over visits, installation of naval communication equipment and its reclamation plans, all of which to be the evidence of *effectivitès*[14].

The definition of "*effectivitès*" is first brought up in the case of frontier dispute in the context of "colonial *effectivitès*" referring to the conduct of the administrative authorities as proof of the effective exercise of territorial jurisdiction in the region during the colonial period. ICJ mentioned below and this shows the usage of the "*effectivitès*" in the context of a sovereignty dispute.

> "a distinction must be drawn among several eventualities...The role played in this case by such *effectivités* is complex, and the Chamber will have to weigh carefully the legal force of these in each particular instance. It must however state forthwith, in general terms, what legal relationship exists between such acts and the titles on which the implementation of the principle of *uti possidetis* is grounded. For this purpose, a distinction must be drawn among several eventualities. Where the act corresponds exactly to law, where effective administration is additional to the *uti possidetis juris*, the only role of *effectivité* is to confirm the exercise of the right derived from a legal title. Where the act does not correspond to the law, where the territory which is the subject of the dispute is effectively administered by a State other than the one possessing the legal title, preference should be given to the holder of the title. In the event that the *effectivité* does not co-exist with any legal title, it must invariably be taken into consideration. Finally, there are cases where the legal title is not capable of showing exactly the territorial expanse to which it relates. The *effectivité* can then play an essential role in showing how the title is interpreted in practice" [15].

14) (Malaysia vs. Singapore), ICJ Reports (2008), p.87, para 274.
15) (Burkina Faso vs. the Republic of Mali), ICJ Reports (1986), p. 587, para. 63.

2. East Timor Case[16)]

Key Principle: ICJ can only exercise jurisdiction over a State with a consent

1) Facts

Indonesia was colonized by Imperial Netherland and the Netherland company with armed forces or VOC in almost 350 years which then Indonesia proclaimed their Independence on August 17, 1945. Under an International Law Principle of *Uti Posidentis*[17)], West Papua then in 1969 officially was recognized as part of Indonesia after the issuance of United Nations General Assembly Resolution[18)] No. 2504 on November 19, 1969. This resolution gave recognition that West Guinea (Papua) is a part of Indonesia[19)].

For East Timor, Indonesia occupied Timor Leste in 1975. United Nations General Assembly Resolution No. 3485 (XXX) in December 1975[20)], Security Council Resolution No. 384 in December 1975[21)] and Security Council Resolution No. 389 in April 1976[22)] delegitimated

16) Case Concerning East Timor (Portugal v. Australia), Judgement of 30 June 1995, ICJ Report 1995.

17) Appellate Body Reports, US – Tuna II (Mexico), para. 215; US – COOL, para. 271; and US – Tuna II (Mexico) (Article 21.5 – Mexico), para. 7.26. See also Panel Reports, US – Tuna II (Mexico) (Article 21.5 – Mexico), para. 7.73; and US – COOL (Article 21.5 – Canada and Mexico), paras. 7.60-7.62.

18) UN General Resolution is not a formal text and generally not-binding. Resolutions made under Chapter VII are binding in terms of legal status.

19) See United Nation General Assembly no.2504 November 19, 1969.

20) A resolution referred to Portugal "as the administering Power" and called upon "to continue to make every effort to find a solution by peaceful means"; and "strongly deplore[d] the military intervention of the armed forces of Indonesia in Portuguese Timor". Case Concerning East Timor (Portugal v. Australia), ICJ Report 1995.

21) A resolution called upon "all States to respect the territorial integrity of East Timor as well as the inalienable right of its people to self-determination"; "the Government of Indonesia to withdraw without delay all its forces from the Territory"; and further called upon "the Government of Portugal as administering Power to CO-operate fully with the United Nations so as to enable the people of East Timor to exercise freely their right to self-determination". *Ibid.*, para 15.

22) A resolution called upon "the Government of Indonesia to withdraw without further delay all its forces from the Territory"; and further called upon "all States and other parties concerned to CO-operate fully with the United Nations to achieve a peaceful solution to the existing situation".

Indonesia's occupation in East Timor[23]. Australian Minister for Foreign Affairs made it clear that the incorporation of East Timor as part of Indonesia was not recognized by Australia *de facto* on January 20, 1978 when the Minister stated "The Government has made it clear publicly that its opposition to the Indonesian intervention and has made this known to the Indonesian Government" [24]. Then the Minister made a different statement saying that "we recognize the fact that East Timor is a part of Indonesia, but not by which this was brought about" on February 23, 1978[25]. On December 15, 1978, the Australian Minister for Foreign Affairs declared the starting of the negotiation with the Indonesian government for the delimitation of the continental shelf between Australia and East Timor with a statement of "this action will signify *de jure* recognition by Australia of the Indonesian incorporation of East Timor"[26].

Australia argued that this case requires the Court to rule on the lawfulness of the conduct of a third country, in this case, Indonesia, in the absence of that State's consent. Australia initially argued that there is no dispute between Portugal and Australia. Since Indonesia did not accept the compulsory jurisdiction of ICJ under Art.36, paragraph 2 of its Statute, Portugal could not bring Indonesia to ICJ unless there was a consent to making Australia responsible instead. East Timor is now an Independent state following an UN-administered transition period, East Timor is internationally recognized as an independent nation on May 20, 2020.

23) Withdrawal of portuguese authorities and occupation by Indonesian armed forces in the East Timor territory in 1975, the question of East Timor became the subject of two resolutions of the Security Council and of eight resolutions of the General Assembly. Security Council resolutions 384 (1975) of 22 December 1975, 389 (1976) of 22 April 1976, General Assembly resolutions 3485 (XXX) of 12 December 1975, 31/53 of 1 December 1976, 32/34 of 28 November 1977, 33/39 of 13 December 1978, 34/40 of 21 November 1979, 35/27 of 11 November 1980, 36/50 of 24 November 1981 and 37/30 of 23 November 1982. *Ibid.*, para 11.

24) Case Concerning East Timor (Portugal v. Australia), Judgement of 30 June 1995, ICJ Report 1995. para 17.

25) *Ibid.*

26) *Ibid.*

2) Court Decision

In the East Timor case, ICJ concluded that:

> "35...the Court would necessarily have to rule upon the lawfulness of Indonesia's conduct as a prerequisite for deciding on Portugal's contention that Australia violated its obligation... However, in this case, the effects of the judgment requested by Portugal would amount to a determination that Indonesia's entry into and continued presence in East Timor are unlawful and that, as a consequence, it does not have the treaty-making power in matters relating to the continental shelf resources of East Timor. Indonesia's rights and obligations would thus constitute the very subject matter of such a judgment made in the absence of that State's consent. Such a judgment would run directly counter to the "well-established principle of international law embodied in the Court's Statute, namely, that the Court can only exercise jurisdiction over a State with its consent[27)]"

In the case of Monetary Gold Removed from Rome in 1943, ICJ ruled that, in the absence of Albania's consent, it could not make any decision on the international responsibility of that State since "Albania's legal interests would not only be affected by a decision but would form the very subject-matter of the decision"[28)]. The ICJ confirms the decision in several cases after Monetary Gold case, such as Military and Paramilitary Activities in and against Nicaragua[29)], Jurisdiction and Admissibility, Judgment of

27) *Ibid.* para. 35.
28) (Italy v. France, United Kingdom of Great Britain and Northern Ireland and Unites States of America), ICJ Reports 1954, p. 32.
29) (Nicaragua v. United States of America), ICJ Reports 1984, p. 431, para. 88.

Frontier Dispute[30]; Land, Island and Maritime Frontier Dispute[31]; and Certain Phos- phate Lands in Nauru[32].

Furthermore, in para 36 and 37, ICJ stated that:

"36. Having dismissed the first of the two objections of Australia which it has examined, but upheld its second, the Court finds that it is not required to consider Australia's other objections and that it cannot rule on Portugal's claims on the merits, whatever the importance of the questions raised by those claims and of the rules of international law which they bring into play (36)"

"37. The Court recalls in any event that it has taken note in the present Judgment (paragraph 31) that, for the two Parties, the Territory of East Timor remains a non-self-governing territory and its people has the right to self-determination. Which the decision was in favour of Australia but then in Paragraph 31 The Court reminds that the people of East Timor had right of Self-Determination following Internation decision like the Security Council, in its resolutions 384 (1975) and 389 (1976) has expressly called for respect for "the territorial integrity of East Timor as well as the inalienable right of its people to self-determination in accordance with General Assembly resolution 1514 (XV)".

3) Comments

(1) Self-Determination

Self-determination of the people is included in UN Charter Art.1(2) as one of the purposes of the UN by stating that "To develop friendly

30) (Burkina Faso/Republic of Mali), Judgment, ICJ Reports 1986, p. 579, para. 49.

31) (El Salvador/Honduras), Application to Intervene, Judgment, ICJ Reports 1990, pp. 114-1 16, paras. 54-56, and p. 112, para.73.

32) (Nauru v. Australia), Preliminary Objections, Judgment, ICJ Reports 1992, pp. 259-262, paras. 50-55.

relations among nations based on respect for the principle of equal rights and self-determination of peoples, and to take other appropriate measures to strengthen universal peace". Also, in International Covenant on Civil and Political Rights(ICCPR) as a political right. It is stated in Article I verse 1 and 3 of ICCPR that said[33] "All peoples have the right of self-determination. By virtue of that right, they freely determine their political status and freely pursue their economic, social, and cultural development.[34] The States Parties to the present Covenant, including those having responsibility for the administration of Non-Self-Governing and Trust Territories, shall promote the realization of the right of self-determination, and shall respect that right, in conformity with the provisions of the Charter of the United Nations[35]."

After much dispute on the interpretation of self-determination, the Committee on the Elimination of Racial Discrimination provided a general comment on the self-determination. It said "4. In respect of the self-determination of peoples, two aspects have to be distinguished. The right to self-determination of people has an internal aspect, that is to say, the rights of all peoples to pursue freely their economic, social and cultural development without outside interference...The external aspect of self-determination implies that all people have the right to determine freely their political status and their place in the international community based upon the principle of equal rights and exemplified by the liberation of peoples from colonialism..."[36].

(2) The Obligation of *Erga Omnes*

"*Erga Omnes*" means "flowing to all" in Latin. UN third report on state

33) International Covenant on Civil and Political Rights 1966 (ICCPR).
34) ICCPR Article 1 Verse 3.
35) *Ibid.*
36) Kim, Dae-Soon, *International Law, 17th* Ed. Samyoungsa, p.407, FN105.

responsibility written by James Crawford distinguishes 'bilateral obligation' and 'multilateral obligation'. Then he separates multilateral obligation into 'obligation *erga omnes*' and 'obligation *erga omnes* partes'. He explains that "obligation *erga omnes* is an obligation owed to the international community as a whole" and its scope is equal to the preemptory obligation that is '*Jus cogens*'[37)38)].

In the Barcelona Traction case, ICJ stated that "...an essential distinction should be drawn between the obligations of a State towards the international community as a whole, and those arising *vis-à-vis* another State in the field of diplomatic protection. By their very nature, the former is the concern of all States. Because of the importance of the rights involved, all States can be held to have a legal interest in their protection; they are obligations *erga omnes*". Then ICJ provided examples where *erga omnes* obligation can be found by emphasizing the basic rights of the human person that "Such obligations derive, for example, in contemporary international law, from the outlawing of acts of aggression, and genocide, as also from the principles and rules concerning the basic rights of the human person, including protection from slavery and racial discrimination. Some of the corresponding rights of protection have entered into the body of general international law (*Reservations to the Convention on the Prevention and Punishment of the Crime of Genocide, Advisory Opinion, I.C.J. Reports 1951, p. 23*); others are conferred by international instruments of a universal or quasi-universal character..."[39)]. Here, ICJ mentioned that an example of genocide is now part of general international law.

---

37) James Crawford, Third Report on State Responsibility (UN doc. A/CN.4/507, 10 March 2000), paras. 99-108.

38) Eun-bum Choe, Jihyun Park, "International Humanitarian Law and Erga Omnes-Focus on Ensuring Respect for International Humanitarian Law-, *The Korean Journal of Humanitarian Law*,Vol.27, 2007.9. pp.27~33.

39) Barcelona Traction case (Belgium v Spain) (Second Phase), ICJ Reports (1970) Paras 33-34.

In Nuclear Test case, the Court also mentions *erga omnes* obligation on the action taken by France promising to the world that the France will not the conduct nuclear test near the islands anymore. ICJ stated that "The unilateral statement of the French authorities were made outside the Court, publicly and *erga omnes*....The general nature and characteristics of these statements are decisive for the evaluation of the legal implication..." by interpreting it even if the action taken by France is unilateral declaration, it was done to the international community as a whole then there is a legal undertaking[40]. In Western Sahara case, ICJ stated that "Self-determination requires a free and genuine expression of the will of the people concerned". The principle of self-determination of the people is *jus cogens* and an obligation *erga omnes*[41].

40) Nuclear Tests case (New Zealand v. France), Judgement, ICJ Reports 1974, paras.52, 58-59.
41) Western Sahara case, ICJ Advisory Opinion, ICJ Reports 1975, paras.54-59.

3. Sinking Illegal Fishing Vessels in Indonesia

Key Principle: Although the exercise of sovereign rights should confirm with international standards, state sovereignty reaches over the territorial sea, continental shelf and EEZ for the matter of right to hot pursuit

1) Facts

Two-thirds of the territory of the Republic of Indonesia is the sea (5.8 million km) and in terms of coastline length, it is the second largest in the world (95,181 km)[42]. For decades, fishing vessels from neighboring countries have rather freely caught fish in Indonesia. Indonesian losses by illegal fishing have been calculated by the World Bank and the FAO (Food and Agriculture Organization) and it is approximately 20 billion US dollars or valued at Rp 240 trillion per year (assuming Rp 12,000 per US dollar). One vessel fish caught without a permit with a capacity of 100 Gross Tons (GT) can make a profit of 2-2.5 million US dollars per year because they catch not only tuna, but also shellfish, sea cucumbers, and lobsters[43].

Not only that the massive catching of fish by foreign vessels but also the use of nott environmentally friendly tools even tend to damage nature. It has made the most of Indonesia's waters in critical condition[44]. To make matters worsen, BPS (Statistics Indonesia) survey for the period 2003 - 2013 shows, the number of fishing households have also decreased from 1.6 million to only around 800,000. Also, as many as 115 national fish processing companies went out of business because of not getting enough fish supplies partially because fishes illegally caught were

42) Kementerian dan Kelautan dan Perikanan Republik Indonesia, *Laut Masa Depan Bangsa*, Jakarta, Kementerian dan Kelautan dan Perikanan Republik Indonesia, p.28.
43) Kementerian dan Kelautan dan Perikanan Republik Indonesia, *Laut Masa Depan Bangsa*, Jakarta, Kementerian dan Kelautan dan Perikanan Republik Indonesia, p.13.
44) *Ibid*, p.13.

processed abroad[45]. Due to the seriousness of this condition, President Jokowi created Task Force 115 consisting of the Indonesian Navy, the National Police, BAKAMLA (Indonesian Maritime Security Agency) and the Attorney General's Office of the Republic of Indonesia, thereby facilitating coordination, encouraging coordination synergy and carrying out the facilitation function in combating illegal fishing to achieve fair law enforcement and provide a deterrent effect[46].

As of April 2017, Task Force 115 had sunk 317 illegal fishing vessels. Out of the total sunken vessels, 296 vessels are foreign-flagged and those vessels belong to Vietnam (142), Philippines (76), Malaysia (50), and Thailand (21), Papua New Guinea (2), China (2), Belize (2), and one fish vessel marked without nationality. Meanwhile, 21 Indonesian-flagged vessels were also sunken[47]. One of the many cases that was brought to the Tanjungpinang District under Court Number 4/PID. SUS-PRK/2014/PN TPG when Thai Ship caught by Indonesia Task Force 115 resulted in the sinking of the ship.

2) Court Decision

The Judge of Panel at the Tanjungpinang Fisheries District Court handed down a criminal sentence to the defendant Mr. Sangwiam Srisom who is a Thai citizen with a vessel called KM. SEA NATUNA 28 alias KM. SUDHITA. He was sentenced to 3 (three) years imprisonment, a fine of Rp.500,000,000 (five hundred million rupiahs), stipulating imprisonment for 3 (three) months for non-payment of fine. Indonesia has confiscated evidence for the state in the form of 1(one) KM vessel unit, SEA NATUNA 28 with its contents.

45) *Ibid*, p.19.
46) *Ibid*, p.21.
47) *Ibid*, p.41.

3) Comments

(1) Territorial of Sea

Under the United Nations Convention on the Law of the Sea 1982 or UNCLOS 1982, a country had 3 layers of sea territory, first is the territorial sea, UNCLOS 1982 described the Territorial Sea as[48]:

> "The sovereignty of a coastal State extends, beyond its land territory and internal waters and, in the case of an archipelagic State, its archipelagic waters, to an adjacent belt of sea, described as the territorial sea."

The next is the Continental Shelf that UNCLOS 1982 described as[49]:

> "The continental shelf of a coastal State comprises the seabed and subsoil of the submarine areas that extend beyond its territorial sea throughout the natural prolongation of its land territory to the outer edge of the continental margin, or to a distance of 200 nautical miles from the baselines from which the breadth of the territorial sea is measured where the outer edge of the continental margin does not extend up to that distance."

And the last is Exclusive Economic Zone that UNCLOS 1982 describes as[50]:

> "The exclusive economic zone is an area beyond and adjacent to the territorial sea, subject to the specific legal regime established in this Part, under which the rights and jurisdiction of the coastal State and the rights and freedoms of other States are governed by the relevant provisions of this Convention."

48) Article 2(1) of United Nations Convention on the Law of the Sea 1982.
49) Article 55 of United Nations Convention on the Law of the Sea 1982.
50) *Ibid.*

A country then has a right to enforce the national law within the territory. UNCLOS Chapter III states the right to hot pursuit.

(2) Right of Hot Pursuit

UNCLOS 1982 defined Hot Pursuit as[51]:

> "The hot pursuit of a foreign ship may be undertaken when the competent authorities of the coastal State have good reason to believe that the ship has violated the laws and regulations of that State. Such pursuit must be commenced when the foreign ship or one of its boats is within the internal waters, the archipelagic waters, the territorial sea or the contiguous zone of the pursuing State, and may only be continued outside the territorial sea or the contiguous zone if the pursuit has not been interrupted. It is not necessary that, at the time when the foreign ship within the territorial sea or the contiguous zone receives the order to stop, the ship giving the order should likewise be within the territorial sea or the contiguous zone. If the foreign ship is within a contiguous zone, as defined in article 33, the pursuit may only be undertaken if there has been a violation of the rights for the protection of which the zone was established"

There are special measurements that can be taken by the nation when its territory is being violated. Is the sinking of the illegal fishing vessel justifiable by the law? As long as the measure taken by the authority fits the treaty clause[52] as well as national law, action can be justifiable.

51) Article 111 of UNCLOS 1982.

52) UNCLOS Art. 21(1) The coastal state may adopt laws and regulations, in conformity with the provisions of this convention and other rules of International law, relating to innocent passage through the territorial sea, in respect of all or any of the following: (e) the prevention of infringement of the fisheries laws and regulations of coastal state.
UNCLOS Art. 73 (1) The coastal State may, in the exercise of its sovereign rights to explore, exploit, conserve and manage the living resources in the exclusive economic zone, take such measures, including boarding, inspection, arrest and judicial proceedings, as may be necessary

(3) Special Measurement

Indonesia's dismissal of foreign illegal ships is justified under Article 69 (4) Law No.45/2009 on fishery, Indonesia and this states[53]:

> "In carrying out the functions referred to in paragraph (1) fisheries investigators and / or supervisors can take special measures in the form of arson and/or sinking of foreign-flagged fishing vessels based on sufficient preliminary evidence."

According to the article of law, Indonesia seems to have the right to burn foreign illegal fish boats. Furthermore, Jawahir Thontowi stated that Indonesia's geographical, geopolitical, sociological status made it harder to facilities and make infrastructures for enforcement of the law. It is justified for Indonesia to create a shock therapy to show how serious the Indonesian government is in enforcing its law[54].

---

to ensure compliance with the laws and regulations adopted by it in conformity with this Convention (2) Arrested vessels and their crews shall be promptly released upon the posting of reasonable bond or other security (3) Coastal State penalties for violations of fisheries laws and regulations in the exclusive economic zone may not include imprisonment, in the absence of agreements to the contrary by the States concerned, or any other form of corporal punishment (4) In cases of arrest or detention of foreign vessels the coastal State shall promptly notify the flag State, through appropriate channels, of the action taken and of any penalties subsequently imposed.

53) Article 69 (4) of Law No. 45/2009 on Fisheries.

54) Jawahir Thontowi, Pembakaran dan Penenggelaman Kapal Nelayan Asing dalam Perspektif Hukum Laut Nasional dan Internasional, Pandecta Journal Volume 12. Nomor 2. December 2017, p.12.

Part II

World Trade Organization Cases

4. DS484: Brazil – Indonesia (Halal case)

5. DS467: Indonesia – Australia
   (Tobacco Plain Packaging case)

6. DS312: Indonesia – South Korea (Certain Paper case)

7. DS480: Indonesia – European Union (Biodisel case)

8. DS406: Indonesia – United States
   (Clove Cigarettes case)

9. DS496: Vietnam – Indonesia
   (Iron or Steel Products case)

II World Trade Organization Cases

4. DS484: Brazil – Indonesia (Halal Dispute)

Key Principle: Requiring positive list that rules out certain food products is inconsistent with Art. XI GATT 1994[55]. Halal labeling requirement, having surveillance and implementation of halal slaughtering, was within the meaning of Article III: 4 of the GATT 1994 not reaching to the less favorable treatment

Complaint: Brazil	Respondent: Indonesia
Third Parties (original proceedings):	United States; European Union; Japan; Korea, Republic of; China; Chile; New Zealand; Norway; Viet Nam; Paraguay; Chinese Taipei; India; Australia; Argentina; Russian Federation; Canada; Thailand; Oman; Qatar
Agreements cited: (as cited in panel request)	Art. XI:1 GATT 1994 Art. 4.2 Agriculture Art. 2.2, 3.1, 3.2, 3.3, 5.1, 5.2, 5.4, 5.6, 8, Annex C Sanitary and Phytosanitary Measures (SPS) Art. 2.2 Technical Barriers to Trade (TBT) Art. 3.2, 3.3 Import Licensing Art. 2.3 Sanitary and Phytosanitary Measures (SPS) Art. 2.1 Technical Barriers to Trade (TBT) Art. III:4, X:3 GATT 1994 Art. 7, Annex B Sanitary and Phytosanitary Measures (SPS)

Consultations requested	: 16 October 2014
Panel requested	: 15 October 2015
Panel established	: 3 December 2015
Panel composed	: 3 March 2016
Panel report circulated	: 17 October 2017 (adopted on 22 November 2017)

1) Facts

In 2014, Indonesia enacted Law No.33/2014 Halal Product Certification which covers halal certification systems for all food, beverage, drugs, cosmetics, chemicals (used for human consumption), organic and

55) Jawahir Thontowi, Pembakaran dan Penenggelaman Kapal Nelayan Asing dalam Perspektif Hukum Laut Nasional dan Internasional, Pandecta Journal Volume 12. Nomor 2. December 2017, p.12.

genetically modified products sold in Indonesia as well as the machinery and equipment processing these products. Indonesia initially adopted the halal product certification system in 1989[56]. Slowly, the certificate system of Indonesia became stricter to reach the trade-restrictive measure prohibiting imported foreign products. Brazilian chicken meat and chicken products into Indonesia had dropped to almost zero since 2006 (chicken cuts), and 2009 (whole chicken).

2) Court Decision

Brazil made claims against two categories of measures: first, an alleged (unwritten) general prohibition resulting from the combined operation of several different trade-restrictive measures (constitutive elements); second, six individual trade-restrictive measures pertaining to the i) non-inclusion of certain chicken products ii) the limitation of imports of chicken meat and chicken products to certain intended uses iii) undue delay in the approval of veterinary health certificates for chicken products from Brazil iv) import licensing regime v) surveillance and implementation of halal slaughtering and labeling requirements for imported chicken meat and chicken products established by different Indonesian regulations vi) restrictions on the transportation of imported products by requiring direct transportation from the country of origin to the entry points in Indonesia. These measures at issue were continuously remanded through new law during the dispute process resulting in the new set of written submission by Brazil.

56) Research conducted by LPPOM MUI, NGO in 1988 showed that some food products in the public contained pork's DNA. After this discovery, the official entity LPPOM MUI since 1989 in collaboration with MUI Fatwa Commission conducted a task of deciding the nature of the product. However in 1996, when Food Act No. 7 of 1996 came into existence, the authority of LPPOM MUI was not designated examining authority by the law. After when the Decree of the Minister of Religious Affairs No. 518 of 2001 on Guidelines and Procedures for the Inspection and Determination of Halal Food was issued, Indonesia moved from a voluntary LPPOM MUI certification system to mandatory BPJPH in 2014.

(1) Non-inclusion of certain chicken products using "positive list requirement", qualify as a 'legal ban' and was inconsistent with Article XI of the GATT 1994. When the Panel assessed with the "weighing and balancing all factors" of the "necessity test" under Article XX(d) of the GATT 1994, the Panel found that this measure was not justified under Article XX of the GATT 1994. Although the Indonesian government remanded the law twice during the WTO process, the measure did not cease to exist and continues to apply in the same manner;

(2) The measure "intended use requirement (limitation of imports of chicken meat and chicken products to certain intended uses), the Panel found that this measure operates as a restriction on imports within the meaning of Article XI of the GATT 1994 and is not justified under Article XX of the GATT 1994. Requiring the chicken to be sold in places with cold storage facilities is not itself inconsistent with Article III:4 of the GATT 1994. However, the provisions concerning the measure's enforcement were also concluded as enforcement provision that made a competitive disadvantage for imported products breaching Article III:4 and not justified under the Article XX(b) of the GATT 1994;

(3) Indonesia's import licensing regime, having a single measure consisting of the application windows and the validity periods, is inconsistent with Article XI:1 of the GATT 1994 and not justified under Article XX(d) of the GATT 1994. But the panel was no longer able to issue a recommendation because, during the process, a single measure consisting of the application window and the validity period had expired. When Indonesia enacted the third set of halal law, Brazil had failed to make a prima facie case. Allowing limited port of entry and the quantity of imported products is also inconsistent

with Article XI:1 of the GATT 1994 which is not in the scope of XX of the GATT;

(4) The undue delay caused by the approval of the veterinary health certificate which contains non-SPS questionnaires (that seems to be information relating to halal assurances) is inconsistent with Article 8 and Annex C(1)(a) of the SPS Agreement;

(5) Halal labeling requirement, having surveillance and implementation of halal slaughtering, was within the meaning of Article III: 4 of the GATT 1994 not reaching to the less favorable treatment;

(6) With respect to the transportation requirement, Brazil was not successful in demonstrating how the measure constituted a violation of Article XI of the GATT 1994 or Article 4.2 of the Agreement on Agriculture.

Altogether, Brazil's claim on the Indonesian halal law containing the general prohibitions for the purpose of self-sufficiency was not proven fully, certain measures are found to be trade-restrictive which requires a revision of the law.

3) Comments

(1) Non-Tariff Measures (NTMs)

A non-tariff barrier is any measure, other than a customs tariff, that acts as a barrier to international trade. The UN Conference on Trade and Development classified 16 non-tariff barriers in 2012.

Imports technical measures	A sanitary and phytosanitary measures B technical barriers to trade C pre-shipment inspection and other formalities
Imports non-technical measures	D contingent trade protective measure E non-automatic licensing and quantity control measures F price control measures, additional taxes and charges G finance measures H measures affecting competition I trade-related investment measures J distribution restrictions K restriction on post-sales services L subsidies M government procurement restrictions N Intellectual property O rules of origin
Export measures	P export-related measures

(2) Technical Barrier

Exporting companies must sometimes incur additional costs as they adapt their production to the changing legal requirements of the recipient country. Such requirements can thus create technical barriers to trade. Discrepancies between product rules adopted by different countries can involve numerous aspects: weight, size, packaging, ingredients, mandatory labeling, shelf-life conditions, testing and certification procedures, etc. These can be the barrier.

Therefore, under the TBT Agreement, there are two categories of rules which should be notified:

(1) Technical regulations that lay down mandatory product characteristics

or their related processes and production methods. For example, requirements on product size, weight, composition, packaging, marking, labeling;

(2) Conformity assessment procedures that are any procedure used to determine whether the relevant requirements of technical regulations or standards are fulfilled. For example, procedures for sampling, testing, inspection, evaluation, verification and assurance of conformity, registration, accreditation, and approval.

(3) Three-tier Test to Interpret "Technical Regulation"

TBT Art. 2.1. states no less favorable treatment on technical regulation. Annex 1 articulates the definition of technical regulations as "a document which lays down product characteristics or their related processes and product methods, including the applicable administrative provisions, with which compliance is mandatory. It may also include or deal exclusively with terminology, symbols, packaging, marketing or labeling requirements as they apply to a product, process or production method". EC-Asbestos case[57)] and EC-Sardines case[58)] Appellate Body used three-tier test in addition to the examination as a whole[59)].

The three-tier test consists first, the document must apply to an identifiable product or group of products. Second, the document must lay down one or more characteristics of the product. These product characteristics may be intrinsic, or they may be related to the product.

57) Panel Report, European communities-Measures Affecting Asbestos and Asbestos-containing Products, WT/DS135/R, Sep. 18, Appellate Body Report, European Communities-Measures Affecting Asbestos and Asbestos-containing Products, WT/DS/135/AB/R. AB Body Report, EC Asbestos, para.64, "The measure at issue is to be examined as an integrated whole, taking into account, as appropriate, the prohibitive and the permissive elements that are part of it".

58) AB Body Report, EC-Sardines, para.176.

59) AB Body Report, EC Asbestos, para.64, "The measure at issue is to be examined as an integrated whole, taking into account, as appropriate, the prohibitive and the permissive elements that are part of it".

Third, compliance with the product characteristics must be mandatory.

Applying the technical regulation three-tier test, the first-tier test requires the existence of identifiable products. No.33/2014 concerning halal product assurance applies to "goods and/or services related to food, beverage, medicine, cosmetics, chemical products, biological products, products of genetic engineering, as well as the use of used goods, used or used by the community". Halal food includes milk, honey, seafood, nut products, fruits, grains and slaughtered meats which accords the Muslim commandments. Halal certificate also applies to food and non-food processes and non-food includes medical supplies, cosmetics, and health dietary supplies. Like this, law No.22/2014 applies to an identifiable group of products. The second-tier test requires the existence of characteristics of the products. No.33/2014 lay down one or more characteristics of the 'Halal' products'. The third tier test which requires a mandatory compliance factor is also fulfilled since compliance through HAS (halal assurance system) requiring Jaminan Produk Halal(JPH) with the supervision of Penyedia Halal and Lembaga Pemeriksa Halal(LPH) is explicitly required to complete by a seller in law No. 22/2014.

(4) Like Product

How about applying "like product" determination criteria to Halal? Halal is an Arabic word that translates to "permissible"[60]and Haram means forbidden in contrast to the Halal[61]. Halal certificate system bases the guideline following the teachings of Al-Qur'an, Al-Hadis with interpretation by the fatwa. The EC-seal Appellate Body however concluded that" ...the measures condition market access on the type and purpose of the seal hunt,

60) Halal definition is from Wikipedia.

61) Mustafa Afifi Ab. Halim and Mohd Mahyeddin Mohd Salleh, "The Possibility of Uniformity on Halal Standards in Organization of Islamic Countries (OIC) Country", *World Applied Sciences Journal*, Vol.17, 2012, p.6.

and the identity of the hunter. As we pointed out above, such criteria do not constitute product characteristics in the sentence of Annex 1.1."

In the US – Clove Cigarettes, the Appellate Body endorsed a competition-oriented approach to the "like products" analysis under Article 2.1 of the TBT Agreement and rejected the approach based on the regulatory objectives of a technical regulation[62]. Therefore, the physical characteristics of halal products that seem to have a special procedure to slaughter, certify, display, store is not so different from the physical characteristics of the other products in the market. Remember, any criteria, the standard is viewed from a layman's perspective.

(5) No Less Favorable Treatment

For the analysis on the "less favorable treatment", the US -Tuna II and the US-Cool case analytical approach crystallized into the following two-step assessment of whether the technical regulation at issue accords *de facto* less favorable treatment under Article 2.1: (i) whether the technical regulation modifies the conditions of competition to the detriment of imported products *vis-à-vis* like products of domestic origin and/or like products originating in any other country(effect); and (ii) whether such detrimental impact "stems exclusively from a legitimate regulatory distinction(purpose)". In the US-Cool case, the Appellate Body pointed "intervention of some element of private choice does not relieve [a Member] of responsibility … for the resulting establishment of competitive conditions less favorable for the imported product than for the domestic product". The detrimental impact of the No.33/2014 measure of giving disproportionate burden may lack the even-handedness to different producers resulting in less favorable treatment.

62) Appellate Body Report, US – Clove Cigarettes, paras. 107-120.

(6) More Trade-Restrictive than Necessary

Apply the steps taken when assessing the "more trade-restrictive than necessary" elements within the meaning of TBT Art. 2.2. by the US-Tuna II case, (i) the degree of contribution made by the measure to the legitimate objective at issue; (ii) the trade-restrictiveness of the measure; and (iii) the nature of the risks at issue and the gravity of consequences that would arise from nonfulfillment of the objective(s) pursued by the Member through the measure to come to the conclusion. The LPH appointed auditor requirement of a. Indonesian citizen; b. Muslim; c. minimum education of bachelor's degree in food, chemistry, biochemistry, industrial engineering, biology, or medicine; d. understanding and have a broad insight regarding product halalness according to Islamic sharia; e. prioritizing the people's interests on top of private and/or group interests; and f. obtain a certificate from MUI seem "more trade-restrictive than necessary to fulfill a legitimate object[63)]".

63) Comments in this halal case is covered in detail at Park, Jihyun,"WTO Compatability of Halal Certification- focus on Indonesia-",Yonsei Law Review, Vol.26 No.2, 2016.

5. DS 467 Indonesia-Australia -Tobacco Plain Packaging Case[64]

Key Principle: Elements to measure the likeness of the products, the significance of the toxicity of a subject product is also in relation to consumer behavior and producer

Complaint: Ukraine (DS434), Honduras(DS435) Dominican Republic (DS441), Cuba(DS458) Indonesia(DS467)	Respondent: Australia
Agreements cited: (as cited in panel request) at DS434	Art. 15.1, 15.4, 1.1, 16.1, 16.3, 20, 2.1, 3.1 Intellectual Property (TRIPS) Art. 2.1 Technical Barriers to Trade (TBT) Art. I, III:4 GATT 1994
Agreements cited: (as cited in panel request) at DS435	Art. 20, 16.1, 15.4, 2.1, 24.3, 22.2(b), 3.1 Intellectual Property (TRIPS), Art. 2.1, 2.2 Technical Barriers to Trade (TBT) Art. III:4 GATT 1994,Art. 8, 17 Intellectual Property (TRIPS)
Agreement cited: (as cited in panel request) at DS441	Art. 2.1, 3.1, 15.4, 16.1, 20, 22.2(b), 24.3 Intellectual Property (TRIPS) Art. 2.1, 2.2 Technical Barriers to Trade (TBT) Art. III:4 GATT 1994 Art. 16.1 Intellectual Property (TRIPS)
Agreements cited: (as cited in panel request)at DS 458	Art. 2.1, 3.1, 15.1, 15.4, 16.1, 16.3, 17, 22.2(b), 20, 24.3 Intellectual Property (TRIPS) Art. 2.1, 2.2 Technical Barriers to Trade (TBT) Art. III:4, IX GATT 1994
Agreements cited: (as cited in panel request)at DS 467	Art. 2.1, 2.2 Technical Barriers to Trade (TBT) Art. 1.1, 2.1, 3.1, 15.4, 16.1, 16.3, 20, 22.2(b), 24.3 Intellectual Property (TRIPS) Art. III:4 GATT 1994

DS 434 [65] Consultations requested: 13 March 2012 Panel requested: 14 August 2012 Panel established: 28 September 2014 Panel established: 5 May 2014 Mutually Agreed Solution notified: 30 May 2016	DS 435 [66] Consultations requested: 4 April 2012 Panel requested: 15 October 2012 Panel established: 25 September 2013 Panel established: 5 May 2014 Panel report circulate: 28 June 2018 Appellate Body report circulated: June 2020	DS 458 Consultations requested: 3 May 2013 Panel requested: 4 April 2014 Panel established: 25 April 2014 Panel established: 5 May 2014 Panel report circulate: 28 June 2018 Panel report adopted: 28 August 2018	DS 458 Consultations requested: 3 May 2013 Panel requested: 4 April 2014 Panel established: 25 April 2014 Panel established: 5 May 2014 Panel report circulate: 28 June 2018 Panel report adopted: 28 August 2018	DS 467 Consultations requested: 20 September 2013 Panel requested: 3 March 2014 Panel established: 25 March 2014 Panel established: 5 May 2014 Panel report circulate: une 2018

64) Certain Measures Concerning Trademarks, Geographical Indications and Other Plain Packaging Requirements Applicable to Tobacco Products and Packaging.

1) Facts

In 2011, the Australian Government adopted the Tobacco Plain Packaging Act 2011(commonwealth) (hereinafter "The Act")[67]. The Act contains a plain packaging rule which was an optional measure exampled in the guideline[68] of the WHO Framework Convention on Tobacco Control (hereinafter "the FCTC") [69] aimed at reducing smoking-related disease and death. 5 Countries producing large tobacco products brought a suit at WTO[70].

---

65) Third party for Ukraine are Argentina; Brazil; Canada; Dominican Republic; Ecuador; European Union; Guatemala; Honduras; India; Indonesia; Japan; Korea, Republic of; New Zealand; Nicaragua; Norway; Oman; Philippines; Singapore; Chinese Taipei; Turkey; United States; Uruguay; Zambia; Zimbabwe; Chile; China; Cuba; Egypt; Malaysia; Mexico; Moldova, Republic of; Nigeria; Peru; Thailand; Malawi.

66) Third party for Honduras are Argentina; Brazil; Canada; Chile; China; Cuba; Dominican Republi; European Union; India; Indonesia; Japan; Korea, Republic of; New Zealand; Nicaragua; Nigeria; Norway; Panama; Philippines; South Africa; Chinese Taipei; Thailand; Ukraine; United States; Uruguay; Zimbabwe; Guatemala; Singapore; Guatemala; Malawi; Malaysia; Mexico; Singapore; Turkey; Zambia; Peru; Ecuador.

67) Australia's lead of the legislation on the Plain Packaging Act was followed by France, Ireland, Hungary, Norway, Slovenia and the United Kingdom of Great Britain and Northern Ireland. Korea is expected to adopt it in 2022.

68) Guidelines on the implementation of Art. 11 were adopted at WHO FCTC COP3 in 2008. Art. 11 requires each party, within three years of entry into force of the Convention for that Party, to adopt and implement effective measures to prohibit misleading tobacco packaging and labeling, ensuring that picture depicts warning covering 50% or more (no less than 30%) of the principal display area and hazardous effect with constituents and emission information in domestic language.

69) United Nations, Treaty Series, vol.2302, p.166. The convention was adopted during the 56th World Health Assembly, which took place from 19 to 28 May 2003, at the Palais des Nations, Geneva. Convention went into force on 27 February 2005. 168 countries are signatories and currently have 182 Parties. The Republic of Korea signed the treaty on 21 Jul 2003 and ratified it on 16 May 2005. Indonesia is not a party to this treaty. Summery and a certified copy are available at the website https://treaties.un.org/pages/ViewDetails.aspx?src=TREATY&mtdsg_no=IX4&chapter=9&clang=_en.
WHO FCTC led to the protocol on eliminating the illicit trade of tobacco products.

70) Domestically, one case has brought relating to this measure. *JT International SA v Commonwealth of Australia* [2012] HCA 43(5 October 2012). In addition to that, an arbitration claims under the investor-state dispute settlement regime of the Australia-Hong Kong Agreement on the Promotion and Protection of Investments 1993 was brought to court. *Philip Morris Asia Ltd v The Commonwealth of Australia*, UNICITRAL, PCA Case No. 2012-12. Australia has won it in both cases.

2) Court Decision

The Tobacco Plain Packaging (hereinafter "TPP") measure taken by Australia was upheld at WTO. TPP measure covers the implementation of a wide range of measures suggested by the FCTC. It aimed at curbing the consumption of tobacco products.

Despite the argument of non-applicability of TPP measure to TBT agreement by Australia, the Panel first concluded that the TPP measures are within the definition of technical regulation (Art. 2.2) under the TBT agreement because TPP covers an identifiable group of products with a characteristic requirement which is mandatory[71)]. Then the Panel said that the TPP measures were apt to make a meaningful contribution to Australia's objective of improving public health by reducing the use of as well as exposure to, tobacco products that could result in a "limiting effect on trade". While fulfilling the policy objective is important, the measure should be implemented without resulting in limiting the trade which has to be proved with evidence. On this matter, the actual evidence did not reflect the worry[72)]. Besides the complainants had not demonstrated that the alternative measures suggested by the complaints such as (i) an increase in taxation of tobacco products; (ii) an increase in the minimum legal purchase age for tobacco products; (iii) an improvement of anti-smoking social marketing campaigns; and (iv) the creation of a pre-vetting mechanism for tobacco packaging were less trade-restrictive within the meaning of Art. 2.2, taking into account the nature and gravity of the risks that would arise from the non-fulfillment of Australia's objective. Therefore, the claim on the breach of Art. 2.2 was not successful[73)].

Honduras and Cuba claimed that the TPP measure breached Art. 2.1

71) Panel Report, *Australia – Tobacco Plain Packaging*, para. 7.232.
72) Panel Report, *Australia – Tobacco Plain Packaging,* para. 7.1255.
73) Panel Report, *Australia – Tobacco Plain Packaging,* para. 7.1732.

of TRIPs agreement and Paris Convention Art. 6quinquies (registration of trademarks) by a failure of providing "as is" protection to the duly registered in the country of origin as well as a failure of accepting filing "as is". But the Panel interpreting "protection" as allowing registration and protection under the proper domestic law, conclude that Honduras and Cuba did not demonstrat the argument fully[74].

Honduras, the Dominican Republic, and Cuba also claimed that preventing from using "trademark" for tobacco products created obstacles to the registration of a trademark resulting in the breach of TRIPS Art. 15.4. The Panel pointed that the level of protection given to the Intellectual property right is decided in its territory and the TPP measure did not prevent the registration due to the "nature of the goods or services"[75].

For the matter of TRIPS Art. 16.1, the Panel concluded that the complainants did not demonstrate that the TPP measures were inconsistent with Australia's obligation to allow the owner of a registered trademark to prevent unauthorized use of identical or similar trademarks on identical or similar products, where such use would result in a likelihood of confusion[76].

Also, the Panel concluded that the TRIPS Art.16.3 article supporting the protection of "already well-known trademarks" from the confusion that could arise through reproduction, imitation or translation was not violated due to the TPP measure despite the argument of Cuba and Indonesia because non-use of a trademark in Australia alone does not prevent that particular trademark become well-known[77]outside of Australia.

On the TRIPS Art. 20 issue, "special requirements" of TPP measure was claimed as "encumbrance" to the trade. The Panel used a three-tire test of (i)

---

74) Panel Report, *Australia – Tobacco Plain Packaging*, para. 7.1775.
75) Panel Report, *Australia – Tobacco Plain Packaging*, para. 7.1912.
76) Panel Report, *Australia – Tobacco Plain Packaging*, para. 7.2050.
77) Panel Report, *Australia – Tobacco Plain Packaging*, para. 7.2108.

the nature and extent of the "encumbrance" posed by the "special requirements", (ii) the reasons of special requirements application, (iii) balance between encumbrance and objective in terms of trade restrictiveness was unjustifiable and concluded that the condition applies to all tobacco products not particular products. Therefore, the TPP measures are overall in line with Art. 20 of the TRIPS Agreement[78].

Also, the claim of Paris Convention Art. 10bis (unfair competition) brought by Cuba and Indonesia was not successful in demonstrating unfair competition situation creating confusion within the meaning of para. 3(1)[79] or to engage in acts amounting to misleading indications or allegations within the meaning of para. 3(3)[80]. Honduras, the Dominican Republic, and Cuba did not demonstrate that the TPP measures required market actors to engage in such acts of unfair competition against which Australia was bound to assure effective protection pursuant to para. 1. The Panel gave an opinion that the "act of competition" means "something that is done by a market actor to compete against other actors in the market". Having said that, laws and other instruments that a Member adopts to regulate the market does not *per se* amount to "acts of unfair competition"[81].

Since the GI protection is properly given by Australia, the claim of breach of TRIPS Art. 22.2(b) (use of geographical indications (GIs) constituting unfair competition) claim within the meaning of Paris Convention Art. 10 bis (3)(3) in respect of GIs was not successful either.

3) Comments

(1) Public Health Exception

GATT XX (b) defense using 'public health' has failed in the US-Gaso-

78) Panel Report, *Australia – Tobacco Plain Packaging,* para. 7.2605.
79) Panel Report, *Australia – Tobacco Plain Packaging,* para. 7.2724.
80) Panel Report, *Australia – Tobacco Plain Packaging,* para. 7.2765.
81) Panel Report, *Australia – Tobacco Plain Packaging,* para. 7.2699.

line case in 1996[82], EC-Tariff Preference case in 2004[83], China-Raw Materials in 2010[84], EC-Seal Products in 2012[85], Indonesia-Chicken in 2015[86].

However, in the EC-Asbestos case in 2001[87] although a French ban on the manufacture, importation and exportation and domestic sale and transfer of certain asbestos products including products containing chrysotile asbestos fires, was concluded inconsistent with GATT Article III:4, but justified under Article XXX(b) purposing protecting human life and health[88]. EC-Asbestos case is the first one that weighted regulatory health risk as a crucial factor in terms of like product. In EC-Asbestos, Appellate Body pointed out that XX(b) of the GATT 1994 does not require to *quantify* the risk to human life or health[89].

In Brazil-Retreated Tyres in 2007[90], the Appellate Body upheld the Panel's finding that the import ban was provisionally justified as "necessary" within the meaning of Art. XX(b). "Weighting and balancing" of the relevant factors test were also adopted in this case. The Appellate Body emphasized that the contribution of the 'import ban' in its objectives to achieve protection of human life and health by reducing the risk of escalating dengue fever and malaria from the accumulation of waste tires is 'both vital and important in the highest degree'[91]. Also, in Indonesia-Chicken, the Panel and Brazil agreed with Indonesia that the protection of human health

82) U.S-Standards for Reformulated and Conventional Gasoline, WT/DS2/AB/R.

83) EC-Conditions for the Granting of Tariff Preferences to Developing Countries, WT/DS246/R, WT/DS246/AB/R.(7, April, 2004).

84) China-Measures Related to the Exportation of Various Raw Materials, WT/DS394/AB/R (30, Jan, 2012).

85) EC-Measures Prohibiting the Importation and Marketing of Seal Products, WT/DS400/AB/R, WT/DS401/AB/R (22 May, 2014).

86) Indonesia-Measure Concerning the Importation of Chicken Meat and Chicken Products, WT/DS484/R (17 Oct, 2017).

87) European Communities-Measures Affecting Asbestos and Asbestos-containing Products, WT/DS135/R (12 Mar. 2001).

88) Appellate Body Report, EC – Asbestos, para. 168.

89) Appellate Body Report, EC-Asbestos, para. 167.

90) Appellate Body Report, Brazil – Retreaded Tyres, para. 179.

91) Appellate Body Report, Brazil-Retreaded Tyres, para. 179.

is of "highest importance"[92].

To succeed in XX(b) defense, "no readably available alternative measure" factor, as well as *chapeau* factors, should be fulfilled.

In US-Clove Cigarettes in 2012[93], when applying TBT Art. 2.1, the Appellate Body considered the relevance of physical characteristics and consumer's tastes and habits, competitive relationship as well as the regulatory purpose of health risk associated with a given product as one of the element to measure the likeness of the product(like product test)[94] As a principle, the Appellate Body endorsed a competition-oriented approach rather than aim-and-effect theory to the "like product" analysis under Article 2.1 of the TBT Agreement for a long time[95]. In this case, the Appellate Body criticized the panel for "not taking into all of the relevant criteria"[96]. "After having found that the (degree of) toxicity of a product was a physical characteristic to be taken into account for the determination of likeness under Article III:4, the Appellate Body emphasized the significance of the toxicity of a subject product is also in relation to consumers' behavior"[97]. Then this will also affect the decision process of a producer.

Compare to the general GATT XX, the TBT Agreement does not have *per se* public health exception clause. However, in Art. 2.2 of TBT, relating to the trade-restrictiveness, protection of human health or safety, animal or plant life or health or the environment is listed as a legitimate objective. In cases of US-Cigarettes and Australia-Tobacco, legitimate objective elements are used to justify the measure taken by the government.

92) Panel Report, Indonesia-Chicken, para. 7.225.
93) United States-Measures Affecting the Production and Sale of Clove Cigarettes, WT/DS406/AB/R, April 4, 2012.
94) *Ibid.*, at paras 107-120.
95) *Ibid.*
96) *Ibid.*, para. 109.
97) WTO analytical index GATT Art. 3. pp. 48~49.

(2) Value Battle. IPR right vs. Public Health

Australia-Tobacco case is a landmark case which took a side of public health instead of Intellectual property right. This is a battle of the spear and shield. The first time ever amendment of 1994 WTO/TRIPS Agreement of new article 31 *bis* in 2005 by the General Council decision is also related to the health concern. In fact, 2005 amendment went into force in 2017 since amendment of WTO agreement requires two-thirds of WTO membership. This first amendment accepted in WTO arena was battle of pharmaceutical company's property right v. right to medicine[98]. While there is no provision specifically refer "right to pharmaceuticals", the right to health is firmly grounded in the implications of several international human rights instruments. Public health issue relating to the pharmaceutical patent system was discussed in the Doha round. Given the pressure by third world nations and AIDS activists, November 2001, a WTO Ministerial Conference issued a Declaration[99] clarifying the sovereign power of third world countries to use the flexibility already built into the TRIPs Agreement[100].

Paragraph 6 of the Doha Declaration provides "...WTO members with insufficient or no manufacturing capacities in the pharmaceutical sector could face difficulties in making effective use of compulsory licensing under the TRIPS Agreement. We instruct the Council for TRIPS to find an

98) Below comments are part of the article, Park Jihyun, "Property Right of Pharmaceutical Companies vs. Right of Access to Medicine (Resulted in the First ever Amendment of WTO Agreement)", *Asian International Studies Review*, Vol.8, No.1, April 2007, pp. 31~46.

99) WT/MIN (01)/DEC/2, http://www.wto.org/english/thewto_e/minist_e/min01_e/mindecl_trips_e.htm.

100) TRIPs Agreement does offer some flexibility to developing and least-developed countries with exception clauses and reservation agreement. A practical solution may be found within the system. The terms of WTO/TRIPs Agreement allow at least four exceptions. First, Article 27 of the TRIPs Agreement exclude products from patent protection where necessary to protect public health and the environment; Second, Article 30 create limited exceptions to patents, provided that country can show that the interests of the patent owner are not unreasonably infringed upon; Third, Article 31 allows compulsory licenses to be issued subject to certain restrictions; Fourth, imposing price controls and taxes with no discriminatory standard between domestic and imported goods is also viable under WTO provision.

expeditious solution to this problem and to report to the General Council before the end of 2002." Upon the request to find an expeditious solution for the effective use of compulsory licensing under the TRIPs Agreement, August 30, 2003, an agreement has reached[101]. 2003 decision made it clear regarding waiver provision of the WTO's TRIPs Agreement.

On December 6, 2005, WTO members agreed on an amendment to TRIPs to make a temporary waiver permanent[102]. This General Council decision means the first-time ever amendment of WTO Agreement[103]. Agreeing on the change of the TRIPs agreement on the issue of health concern, an amendment of domestic patent law has followed.

---

101) WT/L/540.

102) WT/L/641, http://www.wto.org/english/tratop_e/trips_e/wtl641_e.htm.

103) The amendment consists of three parts. Article 31 *bis* which is a new addition to the provision. and annex to the TRIPs Agreement and appendix. Article 31 *bis* allow pharmaceutical products made under compulsory licenses to be exported to countries lacking production capacity. It also deals with avoiding double remuneration to the patent owner, regional trade agreements involving least-developed countries, "non-violation" and retaining all existing flexibilities under the TRIPs Agreement. New annex to the TRIPs Agreement set out terms for using the system, and cover definitions, notification, avoiding the pharmaceuticals being diverted to the wrong markets, developing regional systems to allow economies of scale, and annual reviews in the TRIPs An "appendix" to the annex deals with assessing lack of manufacturing capability in the importing country.

6. DS312: Indonesia – South Korea (Korea-Certain Paper)

Key Principle: Trade Commission can use "facts available" in case that companies are not cooperative, or they submit information late when that information to be used to calculate the dumping margin

Complainant: Indonesia	Respondent: Korea, Republic of
Third Parties (original proceedings)	Canada; China; European Communities; Japan; United States; Chinese Taipei
Agreements cited: (as cited in panel request)	Art. 5.4, 2.6, 3.1, 4.1, 5.2, 5.3, 5.7, 12.1.1, 6.5, 6.7, Annex I, Annex II, 6.8, 12.2, 2.1, 2.2, 2.4, 5.8, 9.3, 3.2, 3.4, 3.5, 3.7, 6.1, 6.4, 6.9 Anti-dumping Art. VI:1, VI:2(a), VI:2(b), VI:6 GATT 1994

Consultations requested : 4 June 2004
Panel requested : 16 August 2004
Panel established : 27 September 2004
Panel composed : 25 October 2004
Panel report circulated : 28 October 2005(adopted on 28 November 2005)
Art 21.5 DSU Panel report circulated : 28 September 2007 (adopted on 22 October 2007)

1) Facts

Indonesia as a plaintiff asked World Trade Organization (WTO) to establish a panel against South Korea as a defendant. South Korea initiated the dumping investigation on the dumping of the business information paper and uncoated wood-free printing paper product which is exported to South Korea from Indonesia. 4 companies that are investigated are PT. Indah Kiat Pulp and Paper Tbk ("Indah Kiat"), PT. Pindo Deli Pulp and Paper Mills ("Pindo Deli"), PT Pabrik Kertas Tjiwi Kimia Tbk ("Tjiwi Kimia"), and PT Riau Andalan Kertas ("April Dine").

The Korean Trade Commission (KTC) issued a policy of 3 years' margin dumping on September 24, 2003[104]and imposed definite anti-

104) Korea- Anti-Dumping Duties on Imports of Certain Paper from Indonesia, Report of the Panel, WT/DS312/R, Pg. 2, para. 2.2.

dumping duty of 8.22 percent for the Sinar Mas Grou, i.e. Indah Kiat, Pindo Deli and Tjiwi Kimia as a single exporter and 2.80 percent for April Fine and 2.80 percent for other Indonesian exporters.

Subsequently, the Indonesian government has objected and requested a consultation with South Korea on the matter of Korea's final determination on like products, individual dumping margins, constructed value, treating a certain firm and other firms as a single economic unit; the impact and effect of the dumped imports on the domestic industry and prices in the domestic market, failure to evaluate all relevant economic factors and indices, and denial of access to information.

Indonesia initially wanted to have further discussion on Article IV of GATT 1994, Article XXII:1 of GATT 1994, and Article 17 of ADA[105] etc. which related to the anti-dumping duty imposed on Plain Paper Copier (PPC) and Uncoated Wood-Free Printing Paper (WF) imported from Indonesia and other investigation aspects[106]. However, the consultation failed to resolve the dispute. Therefore, Indonesia submitted an application to establish a Panel to the WTO dispute settlement body (DSB) on August 16, 2004[107].

The meeting was held on 27 September and two parties agreed on an establishment of a panel[108]. The trial was conducted in accordance with

105) During consultation time, Indonesia cited agreement realting to the Art Art. 1, 2.1, 2. 2, 2.4, 2.6, 3.1, 3.2, 3.4, 3.5, 3.7, 4.1, 5.2, 5.3, 5.4, 5.7, 5.8, 6.1, 6.2, 6.4, 6.5, 6.7, 6.8, 6.9 , 6.10, 9.3, 12.1.1, 12.2, AnnexI, AnnexII Anti-dumping, Art. VI:1, VI:2(a), VI :2(b), VI:6 GATT 1994 and at the time of Panel establishment, Indonesia concluded to cite Art. 5.4, 2.6, 3.1, 4.1, 5.2, 5.3, 5.7, 12.1.1, 6.5, 6.7, Annex I, Annex II, 6.8, 12.2, 2.1, 2.2, 2.4, 5.8, 9.3, 3.2, 3.4, 3.5, 3.7, 6.1, 6.4, 6.9 Anti-dumping,Art. VI:1, VI:2(a), VI:2(b), VI:6 GATT 1994.

106) Korea – Anti-Dumping Duties on Imports of Certain Paper from Indonesia, Request for Consultations by Indonesia, WT/DS312/1, G/ADP/D54/1, Para. 1.

107) Korea – Anti-Dumping Duties on Imports of Certain Paper from Indonesia, Request for the Establishment of a Panel by Indonesia, WT/DS312/2, p.1, Para. 3.

108) Korea – Anti-Dumping Duties on Imports of Certain Paper from Indonesia, Constitution of the Panel Established at the Request of Indonesia, Note by the Secretariat, WT/DS312/3, Number 1.

the timetable for the panel and also agreed upon working procedures. On October 28, 2005, the DSB officially issued its panel report. There are four main issues discussed[109]:

(1) Indonesia considers the facts available the KTC have used in calculating margin dumping on the grounds that Indah Kiat, Pindo Deli, and Tjiwi Kimia submitted are cooperative information. Indonesia considers that these actions have violated the provisions of Article 6: 8 and Annex II of the ADA;

(2) Indonesia considers the application of single margin dumping by KTC to three Sinar Mas Group companies base on the status that all three are considered as sole exporters have violated Article 6:10;

(3) Indonesia considers KTC's treatment of PPC and WF as similar products have violated Article 2: 6 ADA; and

(4) Indonesia considers the determination of KTC regarding the causal relationship between the dumping and the losses incurred is judged not based on positive evidence and that is a violatoion of Article 3: 1 ADA.

2) Court Decision

After the entire series of stages in the WB DSB session, the panel report was finally submitted on October 28, 2005 and the following arguments by Indonesia have been granted by the panel, which are:

(1) The Panel found that the KTC did not act inconsistently with Art. 6.8[110]

109) Departemen Perdagangan Republik Indonesia, *op.cit.*, Sidang Panel DSB-WTO Sengketa Dumping Indonesia – Korea, 1-2 Februari 2005 dan 30 Maret 2005 di Jenewa, pp. 3-4.

110) Agreement on Implementation of Article VI of the General Agreement on Tariffs and Trade 1994(ADA) Part I: Art. 6 Evidence 6.8 In cases in which any interested party refuses access to, or otherwise does not provide, necessary information within a reasonable period or significantly impedes the investigation, preliminary and final determinations, affirmative or negative, may be made on the basis of the facts available. The provisions of Annex II shall be observed in the application of this paragraph.

and Annex II (3)[111] when it resorted to facts available for the calculation of normal value for two Indonesian exporters because the information requested (financial statements and accounting records) had not been submitted "within a reasonable period of time";

(2) The Panel found that the KTC acted inconsistently with Art. 6.8 and Annex II (7)[112] in respect of its dumping margin determination for one of the exporters by failing to compare information on a normal value obtained from secondary sources;

(3) KTC has taken actions that are inconsistent with Article 6.7[113] ADA relating to the disclosure of verification results; and

(4) The Panel made it clear that the data submitted to the KT after the deadline were not verifiable within the meaning of Annex II (3) due to the non-cooperation of the companies. Giving notice of its decision to use 'facts available' complies with its obligation under

111) ADA Annex II: Best Information Available in Terms of Paragraph 8 of Art. 6. Annex II (3). All information which is verifiable, which is appropriately submitted so that it can be used in the investigation without undue difficulties, which is supplied in a timely fashion, and, where applicable, which is supplied in a medium or computer language requested by the authorities, should be taken into account when determinations are made. If a party does not respond in the preferred medium or computer language but the authorities find that the circumstances set out in paragraph 2 have been satisfied, the failure to respond in the preferred medium or computer language should not be considered to significantly impede the investigation.

112) ADA Annex II (7). If the authorities have to base their findings, including those with respect to normal value, on information from a secondary source, including the information supplied in the application for the initiation of the investigation, they should do so with special circumspection. In such cases, the authorities should, where practicable, check the information from other independent sources at their disposal, such as published price lists, official import statistics and customs returns, and from the information obtained from other interested parties during the investigation. It is clear, however, that if an interested party does not cooperate and thus relevant information is being withheld from the authorities, this situation could lead to a result which is less favourable to the party than if the party did cooperate.

113) ADA 6.7. In order to verify information provided or to obtain further details, the authorities may carry out investigations in the territory of other Members as required, provided they obtain the agreement of the firms concerned and notify the representatives of the government of the Member in question, and unless that Member objects to the investigation. The procedures described in Annex I shall apply to investigations carried out in the territory of other Members. Subject to the requirement to protect confidential information, the authorities shall make the results of any such investigations available, or shall provide disclosure thereof pursuant to paragraph 9, to the firms to which they pertain and may make such results available to the applicants.

Annex II(6). Also using normal value determination on constructed value under Art. 2.2 due to the non-verifiable data submission by the exports.

3) Comments

(1) Dumping Margin

Dumping is the action taken by the company exporter when an exporting price is lower than the price it normally charges on its own home market for the like products[114] which provides regulation on determination of dumping and evidence that government can use in dumping investigation. Anti-Dumping Agreement (Impenmentation of Article VI of the General Agreement on Tariffs and Trade 1994) regulates how government can or cannot react to dumping and how to calculate dumping margins.

Regarding evidence used at anti-dumping investigation, there are many WTO cases. In this case, Indonesia submitted to the panel that the KTC acted inconsistently with article 6.7 and Annex II(7) ADA by failing to exercise special circumspection in using of information from secondary information. KTC indeed used the secondary information and not from the domestic sales data provided by the two companies. KTC used expenditure data for sales, general and administrative (selling, general and administrative expenses) from Company 'A' and interest expense from Company 'B'. Korea argue that those are the secondary information that has been verified on the investigation period and the data submitted by two companies are not submitted within a given investigation time therefore not verifiable. In calculating financial expenses, KTC used data from the production

114) ADA Part I: Art.2 determination of dumping 2.1. For the purpose of this Agreement, a product is to be considered as being dumped, i.e. introduced into the commerce of another country at less than its normal value, if the export price of the product exported from one country to another is less than the comparable price, in the ordinary course of trade, for the like product when destined for consumption in the exporting country.

Company 'B' as the basis for its calculation. The Panel did not find an explanation why KTC decided to use data from companies whose activities were not the same as related company, such as Company 'B'. The Panel found the KTC acted inconsistently with relevant provisions of the ADA.

Second, it further related with the data used by KTC on article 6.8 of ADA. As the matter of fact, South Korea on its investigation only used the data from KOTIS (Korean Government Custom Statistics), an independent and trusted institution. However, the Panel does not accept evidence that shows information about normal values has been compared with information from other sources that are independent and reliable. The Panel believes that South Korea did not compare the normal value of data with information from other independent and trusted sources because South Korea, as the party who presented the facts, did not provide relevant evidence. Therefore, Panel found that KTC has violated article 6.8 in respect of its dumping margin determination for one of the exporters by failing to compare information on normal value obtained from secondary sources against other independent courses. At the same time, Panel found that KTC has not violated Article 6.8 in respect of its dumping margin determination for two of the exporters because the information requested (financial statements and accounting records) had not been submitted "within a reasonable period of time". The Panel concluded that if the data (on domestic sales) submitted by the exporters is not verifiable, then investigation organization can base its normal value determination on constructed value[115).

115) ADA Art. 2.2 When there are no sales of the like product in the ordinary course of trade in the domestic market of the exporting country or when, because of the particular market situation or the low volume of the sales in the domestic market of the exporting country, such sales do not permit a proper comparison, the margin of dumping shall be determined by comparison with a comparable price of the like product when exported to an appropriate third country, provided that this price is representative, or with the cost of production in the country of origin plus a reasonable amount for administrative, selling and general costs and for profits.

(2) Implementation of Decision

After the recommendation has been issued by the Panel, both parties have agreed upon a specific time to implement the recommendation. Upon the present case, both parties have agreed that the expired time to implement the decision, in this case, shall be in the length of eight months.

According to the recommendation, a country has to revise the regulation. Sometimes one country claim that they are already cooperative in implementing the recommendations but does not revoke the policy that causes the breach, then the other side of the country can actually be considered uncooperative. Then the sunset review which requires automatic withdrawal of the anti-dumping measure taken after 5 years has still applied to the products at this issue. If one does not implement recommendations, the opposite country has a right to compensation or retaliation. South Korea revoked its policy in October 2010.

7. DS480: Indonesia – European Union (Biodiesel Case)

Key Principle: The practice of using "cost" not the "cost prevailing in the country of origin" in the construction of the normal value is inconsistant with Art. 2.2. of ADA

Complainant: Indonesia	Respondent: European Union
Third Parties (original proceedings)	United States; Japan; Turkey; Singapore; India; China; Canada; Argentina; Australia; Norway; Russian Federation; Brazil; Ukraine
Agreements cited: (as cited in panel request)	Art. 2.2, 2.2.1.1 Anti-dumping Art. VI:1 GATT 1994 Art. XVI:4 Agreement Establishing the World Trade Organization Art. 2.2.2(i), 18.4, 2.2.2, 2.2.2(iii), 2.4, 2.3, 9.3, 3.1, 3.4, 3.5, 6.5, 6.5.1, 7.1, 7.2, 9.2, 9.3, 1 Anti-dumping Art. VI GATT 1994

Consultations requested	: 10 June 2014
Panel requested	: 30 June 2015
Panel established	: 31 August 2015
Panel composed	: 4 November 2015
Panel report circulated	: 25 January 2018 (adopted on 28 February 2018)

1) Facts

This case broke out between Indonesia and the European Union (EU) regarding the dumping policy issued by the EU on biodiesel products from Indonesia. After the dumping investigation, European Union imposed anti-dumping measures on Indonesian biodiesel products.

Indonesia is the biggest producer and consumer of the commodity. It provides about half of the world's supply. Europe is one of the biggest consumer markets of Indonesian biodiesel[116)]. Indeed, biodiesel products from Indonesia are fairly cheap. The cheap selling price of palm oil biodiesel sparked the accusations of dumping by other countries[117)].

116) No Author, *Perkembangan Biodiesel Indonesia dan Keberatan Indonesia atas Bea Masuk Anti-Dumping Uni Eropa,* Indonesia Palm Association, last modified october 10, 2019, https://gapki.id/news/2519/perkembangan-biodiesel-indonesia-dan-keberatan-indonesia-atas-bea-masuk-anti-dumping-uni-eropa.

117) Redaksi, *Saatnya Pasar Biodiesel Tumbuh,* Majalah Sawit Indonesia, last modified october 10, 2019, 2019, https://sawitindonesia.com/saatnya-pasar-biodiesel-tumbuh/.

Dumping is said to occur when the goods are exported by a country to another country at a price lower than their normal value and this causes injury to a domestic industry.[118)] This is an unfair trade practice that can have a distortive effect on international trade as it keeps competitors out of a particular market[119)].

In this regard, on 29 August 2012, the European Commission (EC) imposed the measure after an anti-dumping investigation on imports of biodiesel originating from Indonesia (and also Argentina).[120)] After conducting a 15-month investigation by collecting data submitted by the exporters and obtained by the EU, the EU through its commission has enacted an anti-dumping policy. The policy levies extra duties on Indonesian biodiesel by margins of between 8.8 percent and 23.3 percent. (76,94 Euro until 178,85 Euro) per ton[121)]. The Regulation (EU) No.1194/2013 of 19 November 2013 on imposing a definitive anti-dumping duty and collecting definitely the provisional duty imposed on imports of biodiesel originating in Argentina and Indonesia came out through council implementation and Definite Dumping Margain was calculated base on the provisiosns of the Regulation No.1194/2013.

Indonesian government concluded that the EU's measure could give a negative impact on the Indonesian biodiesel exporters and the policy measure imposed by the EU was improper under the ADA. On June 10,

118) K.T Chacko, *FAQ Agreement on Anti-Dumping*, Center for WTO Studies Indian Institute of Foreign Trade, p.1.

119) K.T Chacko, *Op. Cit,* Pg. 1; Muhammad Sood, *Hukum Perdagangan Internasional,* RajaGrafindo, Jakarta, 2011, p.115.

120) Global Trade Alert, *EU: Termination of Definitive Anti-Dumping Duty on Biodiesel Imported from Argentina and Indonesia,* last modified october 10, 2019, https://www.globaltradealert.org/intervention/16654/anti-dumping/eu-termination-of-definitive-antidumping-duty-on-biodiesel-imported-from-argentina-and-indonesia.

121) Council Implementing Regulation (EU) No 1194/2013 of 19 November 2013; Paul Erwin, *What's Wrong With EU biodiesel Anti-Dumping Act?,* The Jakarta Post, last modified october 10, 2019, https://www.thejakartapost.com/academia/2018/03/01/whats-wrong-with-eu-biodiesel-antidumping-act.html.

2014, Indonesia requested consultations with the EU on (a) provisions of Council Regulation (EC) No.1225/2009 on protection against dumped imports from countries not members of the EC; and (b) anti-dumping measures imposed in 2013 by the EU on imports of biodiesel originating in, inter alia, Indonesia[122].

Indonesia claimed that the EU action is not consistent with several agreements, particularly[123]:

(1) Art. 2.2, 2.2.1.1 Anti-dumping;

(2) Art. VI:1 GATT 1994;

(3) Art. XVI:4 of the WTO Agreement;

(4) Art. 2.2.2(i), 18.4, 2.2.2, 2.2.2(iii), 2.4, 2.3, 9.3, 3.1, 3.4, 3.5, 6.5, 6.5.1, 7.1, 7.2, 9.2, 9.3, 1 Anti-dumping;

(5) Art. VI GATT 1994.

Consultations were held on 23 July 2014 but failed to resolve the dispute[124]. After this stage, it enters for the establishment of panels that have been requested by Indonesia on 30 June 2015.[125] At its meeting on 31 August 2015, a panel pursuant to the request of Indonesia was established[126]. Finally, the decision was read on January 25, 2018[127].

122) World Trade Organization, *DS480: European Union — Anti-Dumping Measures on Biodiesel from Indonesia,* last modified October 12, 2019, https://www.wto.org/english/tratop_e/dispu_e/cases_e/ds480_e.htm.

123) *Ibid.*

124) European Union – Anti-Dumping Measures on Biodiesel From Indonesia Report Of The Panel (DS480).

125) World Trade Organization, *DS480: European Union — Anti-Dumping Measures on Biodiesel from Indonesia,* last modified October 12, 2019, https://www.wto.org/english/tratop_e/dispu_e/cases_e/ds480_e.htm.

126) *Ibid.*

127) Kementrian Perdagangan, *Indonesia Menangkan Sengketa Biodiesel dengan Uni Eropa,* Siaran Pers Biro Hubungan Masyarakat, last modified October 5, 2019, www.kemendag.go.id.

2) Court Decision

The Panel made 6 points of findings:[128)]

(1) The EU did not use data that has been submitted by Indonesian exporters in calculating production costs;

(2) The EU did not use data on costs incurred in Indonesia in determining average values for the basis of calculating dumping;

(3) The EU set a limit on profits that are too high for the biodiesel industry in Indonesia and fail to determine "the profit normally realized by other exporters or producers on sales of products of the same general category in the domestic market of the Country of origin.";

(4) The method of determining export prices for one of Indonesia's exporters is not in line with the provisions;

(5) The EU applied taxes that are higher than the dumping;

(6) The EU did not prove that biodiesel imports from Indonesia have a detrimental effect on the price of biodiesel sold by the EU domestic industry. However, Panel did not agree on the claim of excessiveness of the amount of anti-dumping duty imposed. Nor the definte collection of provisional anti-dumping duties on imports for P.T. Musim Mas.

After the adoption of the report by the Panel, the parties concerned must comply with the decision. Both parties agreed to have a reasonable period of time for implementing the DSB's recommendations. The Indonesian government must continue to monitor and coordinate with the producers or exporters to ensure that the EU implements the results of court decisions.

128) World Trade Organization, *DS480: European Union — Anti-Dumping Measures on Biodiesel from Indonesia,* last modified October 15, 2019, https://www.wto.org/english/tratop_e/dispu_e/cases_e/ds480_e.htm.

Now, Indonesia's biodiesel exports are back to compete again in the EU market.

3) Comment

(1) Dumping and Anti-Dumping

Anti-Dumping Agreement, namely Art. VI of GATT 1994, explains in detail the anti-dumping policy that will be issued by the state as a basis to fight dumping practices, including investigations, provisions, and application of dumping fees. In Art. VI, WTO members can provide anti-dumping measures policy after an investigation is carried out in accordance with the agreement, which are[129]:

(1) Dumping has occurred;

(2) Injury within the meaning of Art. VI of GATT 1994 as interpreted exist;

(3) A causal link between the dumped imports and the alleged injury exist.

An anti-dumping investigation is not consistent with ADA if there are only or proven dumping goods and losses suffered by domestic producers. A causal link between a dumping item and a loss (injury) must be shown with relevant, strong, and valid evidence. Proof without a causal link can be considered as insufficient evidence. A causal link is a keyword in an anti-dumping investigation[130].

The burden of proof rests upon the party, whether complaining or defending, who asserts the affirmative of a particular claim or defense[131]. This means that the party claiming a violation of a provision of the WTO

---

129) 1868 U.N.T.S. 201 Art. 5 verse 1.

130) Dewa Gede Pradyana, *Perlindungan Industri Dalam Negeri Dari Praktik Dumping,* Program Pascasarjana Ilmu Hukum Universitas Udayana Denpasar, (2011), p.74.

131) World Trade Organization, *Legal Issues Arising in WTO Dispute Settlement Proceedings,* last modified November 29, 2019 https://www.wto.org/english/tratop_e/dispu_e/disp_settlement_cbt_e/c10s6p1_e.htm#txt1.

Agreement (i.e. the complainant) must assert and prove its claim. In turn, the party invoking in defense with a provision that is an exception to the allegedly violated obligation (i.e. the respondent) bears the burden of proof[132]. Upon the present case, Indonesia as the complainant of such a claim has to prove that the EU acted inconsistently on the article that is applicable. European Union in the opposite, has to prove that the policy applied is a part of the exception under the applicable law.

The measure that the EU has been taken was not based on the assessment of the valid data and measure. The EC used a differential export tax system that applied different tax rates on raw materials and biodiesel. It ruled that the EC should not have taken the view that the price of the raw materials was not reasonably reflected in the records of the Indonesian exporting producers and should not have disregarded those records when constructing a normal value for biodiesel produced in Indonesia.

After the decision has been made by the Panel, the EU had to amend or revoke its regulation on the issue. EU revised a Commission Implementing Regulation (EU) 2018/1570 Of 18 October 2018 Terminating the Proceedings Concerning Imports of Biodiesel Originating in Argentina and Indonesia and Repealing Implementing Regulation (EU) No.1194/2013.

The enactment of new EU regulation will give relief to the Indonesian palm oil industry, as the largest palm producing and exporting country in the world.

---

132) *Ibid.*

8. DS406: Indonesia – United States(Clove Cigarettes)

Key Principle: In TBT 2.1, 2.2, detrimental impact on competitive opportunity for imports that stems exclusively from regulatory distinction is permitted when it only amounts to a less favorable treatment

Complaint: Indonesia	Respondent: United States
Third Parties (original proceedings):	Brazil; Colombia, Dominican Republic; European Union; Guatemala; Mexico; Norway; Turkey
Agreements cited: (as cited in panel request)	Art. III:4, XX GATT 1994 Art. 2.1, 2.2, 2.5, 2.8, 2.9, 2.10, 2.12, 2.3 Technical Barriers to Trade (TBT) Art. 2, 3, 5, 7 Sanitary and Phytosanitary Measures (SPS)

Consultations requested : 7 April 2010
Panel requested : 9 June 2010
Panel established : 20 July 2010
Panel composed : 9 October 2010
Panel report circulated : 2 September 2011 (adopted on 24 April 2012)
Appellate Body report circulated: 4 April 2012 (adopted on 24 April 2012)
Notification of mutually agreed solution: 9 October 2014

1) Facts

Section 907(a)(1)(A) of the United States Federal Food, Drug, and Cosmetic Act ("FFDCA") prohibits the production and sale of cigarettes which contain as a constituent, or additive, an artificial or natural flavor(other than tobacco or menthol) or an herb or spice, including strawberry, grape, orange, clove, cinnamon, pineapple, vanilla, coconut, licorice, cocoa, chocolate, cherry, or coffee by the Family Smoking Prevention and Tobacco Control Act. This Act contains the provision imposing new warnings and labels on tobacco packaging and their advertisement as well as banning flavored cigarettes except tobacco flavor and menthol flavor with the goal of discouraging minors and young adults from smoking.

This Act was signed into law by President Barack Obama. Right after the Act was introduced, Commonwealth Brand filed suit against the United States and the Food and Drug Administration domestically.

Internationally, WTO lawsuit was brought by the clove cigarette producer and importer Indonesia for banning Kreteks (clove cigarettes) not tobacco or menthol flavor which breaches the provisions of WTO Agreements.

2) Court Decision

The Panel found that the measure taken by the U.S. through the Family Smoking Prevention and Tobacco Control Act breached the national treatment obligation of Article 2.1 of the TBT Agreement. The Appellate Body agreed with the conclusion of the panel however with different reasoning.

First, the Panel concluded that menthol-flavored cigarettes and clove flavored cigarettes are "like products" with consideration of "regulatory purpose". However, the Appellate Body rejected the reasoning of the panel[133] and concluded the competitive relationship between the products based the four traditional criteria set in Border Tax Adjustments; (i) the properties, nature, and quality of the products; (ii) the end-uses of the products; (iii) consumer's tastes and habits; (iv) tariff classification of the products[134].

Second, the Appellate Body found the condition of a detrimental impact on competitive opportunity for imports that stems exclusively from legitimate regulatory distinction is permitted[135]. Design, architecture, revealing structure, operation, application of the technical regulation at issue, and, in particular, whether that technical regulation is even-handed

133) Appellate Body Report, US – Clove Cigarettes, paras. 107-120.

134) See, further, Appellate Body Report, Japan – Alcoholic Beverages II, p. 113 and, in particular, fn. 46 See, also, Panel Report, US – Gasoline, para. 6.8, where the approach set forth in the Border Tax Adjustment case was adopted in a dispute concerning Article III:4 of the GATT 1994 by a panel.

135) Appellate Body Report, US – Clove Cigarettes, para. 175.

should be carefully scrutinized. However, the impact on the competitive opportunity for imported clove cigarettes and domestic menthol cigarettes, in this case, amount to a less favorable treatment[136].

Third, the Appellate Body upheld the panel's conclusion on the "reasonable interval" period. When interpreted in the context of paragraph 5.2 of the Doha Ministerial Decision on Implementation-Related Issues and Concerns, a reasonable interval period requires a minimum of six months between the publication and the entry into force of a technical regulation[137]. Since only three months were given to the importers between the publication and the entry into force of the Family Smoking Prevention and Tobacco Control Act, it prima facie proves an act of breach. In reaching this conclusion, the Appellate Body agreed with the Panel that paragraph 5.2 of the Doha Ministerial Decision constitutes a "subsequent agreement between the parties" within the meaning of Article 31(3)(a) of the Vienna Convention on the Law of Treaties[138].

3) Comments

(1) Preamble

The Technical Barrier to Trade(TBT) Agreement has 9 recitals. However, the TBT Agreement does not have an exception clause that GATT has. In this context, the preamble of the TBT plays a role of XX of GATT. Not only that, Panels and the Appellate Body referred to the preamble to the TBT Agreement when interpreting various provisions of the TBT Agreement[139]. Therefore, the preamble of the TBT sets the

136) Appellate Body Report, US – Clove Cigarettes, para. 225.
137) Appellate Body Report, US – Clove Cigarettes, para. 272.
138) Appellate Body Report, US – Clove Cigarettes, para. 290.
139) See Panel Reports, US – COOL (Article 21.5 – Canada and Mexico), para. 7.485; US – Tuna II (Mexico) (Article 21.5 – Mexico), paras. 7.87 and 7.90; EC – Seal Products, paras. 7.416-7.417 and 7.582-7.584; US – COOL, paras. 7.233, 7.551, 7.600, 7.670 and 7.760; US – Tuna

common conditions for all TBT provisions.

(2) Legislative Objective

The sixth recital of TBT reads "Recognizing that no country should be prevented from taking measures necessary to ensure the quality of its exports, or for the protection of human, animal or plant life or health, of the environment, or for the prevention of deceptive practices, at the levels, it considers appropriate, subject to the requirement that they are not applied in a manner which would constitute a means of arbitrary or unjustifiable discrimination between countries where the same conditions prevail or a disguised restriction on international trade, and are otherwise in accordance with the provisions of this Agreement".

In this case, the Appellate Body found that "the explicit recognition of Member's right to regulate"[140]. When the Member pursues "certain legitimate objectives" and measures of technical regulations, standards, and conformity assessment procedure have taken with that legitimate objective keeps the level of appropriateness that is not arbitrary or unjustifiable discriminatory.

The Appellate body concludes "...We thus understand the sixth recital to suggest that Members have a right to use technical regulations in pursuit of their legitimate objectives, provided that they do so in an even-handed manner and in a manner that is otherwise in accordance with the provisions of the TBT Agreement. The balance set out in the preamble of the TBT Agreement between, on the one hand, the desire to avoid creating

II (Mexico), paras. 7.41, 7.110, 7.225, 7.276, 7.460 and 7.467; US – Clove Cigarettes, paras. 7.111-7.114, 7.329, 7.359-7.360, and 7.370; and EC – Sardines, paras. 7.119-7.120. See also Appellate Body Reports, US – COOL (Article 21.5 – Canada and Mexico), paras. 5.201, 5.214, 5.253 and 5.266; US – Tuna II (Mexico) (Article 21.5 – Mexico), paras. 7.30 and 7.87-7.92; EC – Seal Products, paras. 5.121-5.124 and 5.310; US – COOL, paras. 370, 373 and 445; US – Tuna II (Mexico), paras. 212-213, 313, 316 and 379; US – Clove Cigarettes, paras. 89-100, 108-109, 120 and 172-173; EC – Sardines, para. 215.

140) Appellate Body Report, US-Clove Cigarettes (Indonesia), para. 173.

unnecessary obstacles to international trade and, on the other hand, the recognition of Members' right to regulate, is not, in principle, different from the balance set out in the GATT 1994, where obligations such as national treatment in Article III are qualified by the general exceptions provision of Article XX"[141].

The Panel in the *EC-Sardines* mentioned the degree of Member's regulatory autonomy under the TBT agreement[142]. The Appellate Body in the *EC-Tuna II*(Mexico), also considered the sixth recital of the preamble sheds light on the meaning and ambit of the "treatment no less favorable" requirement in Article 2.1[143]. In this sense, the 'purpose' factor that is related to the measure taken should be considered in the context of the "treatment no less favorable" requirement in Article 2.1. It is also important to notice that the Panel in the US – Clove Cigarettes agreed with the parties that the concept of the "level of protection" is related to the question of whether a measure is "more trade-restrictive than necessary" within the meaning of Article 2.2[144].

141) *Ibid.*, paras. 172-174.
142) Panel Report, EC – Sardines, paras. 7.119-7.120.
143) Appellate Body Report, US – Tuna II (Mexico), para. 213.
144) Panel Report, US – Clove Cigarettes, 7.370.

9. DS496: Vietnam – Indonesia(Safeguard on Certain Iron or Steel Products 'Galvalum;)

Key Principle: When a state does not have a binding tariff obligation at WTO schedule of concession for a certain product, one is free to impose any amount of the duty it deems appropriate. However, MFN also applies

Complaint: Viet Nam	Respondent: Indonesia
Third Parties (original proceedings):	United States; European Union; India; Korea, Republic of; Russian Federation; China; Chile; Australia; Japan; Chinese Taipei
Agreements cited: (as cited in panel request)	Art. XIX:1 GATT 1994 Art. 3.1, 2.1, 4.1(a), 4.2(a), 4.2(c), 4.1(b), 4.1(c), 4.2(b) Safeguards Art. I:1 GATT 1994 Art. 12.2 Safeguards Art. XIX:2 GATT 1994 Art. 12.3 Safeguards
Consultations requested: 1 June 2015 Panel requested : 15 September 2015 Panel established : 28 September 2015 Panel composed : 9 December 2015 Panel report circulated: 18 August 2017(adopted on 27 August 2018) Appellate Body report circulated: 15 August 2018(adopted on 27 August 2018)	

1) Facts

Vietnam asked the establishment of a Panel against Indonesia in WTO for the measure taken on imports of certain flat-rolled iron or steel products (Galvalume) in 2015. The Minister of Finance of Republic of Indonesia Regulation No.137.1/PMK.O11/2014 on Implementation of Customs Import Safety Measures Imported Canal Floor Products from Iron or Non-Steel Aloy (Hereinafter Regulation No.137.1/ PMK.O11/2014). Art.1 defines Galvalume as flat-rolled products of iron or non-alloy steel, of a width of 600 mm or more, clad, plated, or coated with aluminum-zinc alloys, containing by weight less than 0.6% of carbon, with a thickness not exceeding 0.7mm, under HS code 7210.61.11.00. Indonesia's competent authority (Komite Pengamanan Perdagangan Indonesia) imposed a specific duty for defined goods for three years starting on 22 July 2014 to 2017.

Indonesia has no binding tariff obligation with respect to galvalume inscribed into its Schedule of Concessions for the purpose of Article II of the GATT 1994. At the time of the request for consultations, the duty rate applied by Indonesia on imports of galvalume on a most-favoured-nation (MFN) basis was 12.5%. This MFN-rate was increased to 20% in May 2015. Indonesia applies duty rates ranging from 0% to 12.5% on imports of galvalume from its trading partners under four separate regional trade agreements (RTAs) – the Association of Southeast Asian Nations (ASEAN)-China Free Trade Agreement (12.5%), the ASEAN-Korea Free Trade Agreement (10%), the ASEAN Trade in Goods Agreement (0%) and the Indonesia-Japan Economic Partnership Agreement (12.5%). The specific duty that is at issue in this proceeding is applied in addition to the existing MFN and preferential duty rates.

Art. 2 of the Regulation No. 137.1/PMK.O11/2014 mentioned that tariff charges 4,998,784 rupiahs ($355) per tonne in the first year, 4,314,161 rupiahs ($308) per tonne in the second year, and 3,629,538 rupiahs ($258) per tonne in the third year between 2014-2017. Because of this increased specific duty, Vietnam and Taiwan asked Panel to interpret the consistency of the measure to the WTO agreement.

With the same regulation, Indonesia applied a special duty to all but 120 countries that were exempt according to the appendix of Regulation No. 137.1/PMK.O11/2014 to afford S&D treatment following the requirements of Article 9.1 of the Safeguard Agreement[145).

145) Art. 9. "1. Safeguard measures shall not be applied against a product originating in a developing country Member as long as its share of imports of the product concerned in the importing Member does not exceed 3 percent, provided that developing country Members with less than 3 percent import share collectively account for not more than 9 percent of total imports of the product concerned".

2) Court Decision

The Appellate Body gave a report and recommendation as follow:

The specific duty applied by Indonesia on imports of galvalume using Regulation No. 137.1/PMK.011/2014 does not constitute a 'safeguard measure' within the meaning of Article 1 of the Agreement on Safeguards[146). However, the application of the specific duty on imports of galvalume originating in all but the 120 countries listed in the appendix of Regulation No. 137.1/PMK.011/2014 is inconsistent with Indonesia's obligation to afford MFN under Article I:1 of the GATT 1947 irrespective of its legal characterization as a safeguard or not[147).

In the light of GATT Art. I:1 Most Favorable Nation Treatment (MFN), the Panel found that the specific duties have nullified or impaired benefits accruing to Chinese, Taipei and Vietnam not others under the GATT 1994. The Panel recommended, according to Article 19.1 of the DSU, that Indonesia bring its measure into conformity with its obligations under Article I:1 of the GATT 1994[148). However, the Panel confirms that Indonesia has no binding tariff obligation with respect to galvalume because that is not listed at WTO Schedule of Concessions. Therefore, Indonesia is free to impose any amount of duty it deemed appropriate on imports of galvalume, including the specific duty at issue in this dispute[149). Accordingly, the Panel found that Indonesia's obligations under Article II of the GATT 1994 did not preclude the application of the specific duty on imports of galvalume, implying that the specific duty did not suspend, withdraw, or modify Indonesia's obligations under Article II of the GATT 1994[150).

146) Panel Report, Indonesia – Safeguard on Certain Iron or Steel Product, WT/DS490/R, WT/DS496/R, and Add.1, Adopted 27 Agustus, as modified by Appellate Body Report WT/DS490/AB/R, WT/DS496/AB/R Para 7.10, p.14.

147) *Ibid*, Para 7.18, p.17.

148) *Ibid*, Para 7.18, p.47.

149) *Ibid*, Para 7.18, p.16.

150) *Ibid*.

The Appellate Body held that, to constitute a safeguard: (i) a measure must suspend in whole or in part a GATT obligation or withdraw or modify a tariff concession; and (ii) the suspension, withdrawal, or modification in question must be designed to prevent or remedy serious injury to a Member's domestic industry caused or threatened by an increase in imports of the subject product[151].

3) Comments

(1) Use of ASEAN Settlement

The only one trade barrier measure Internationally agreed is a tariff. Besides, State can take measures legally under the general exception of Article 20 of GATT if State can properly enforce it without arbitrary or unjustifiable discrimination between countries where the same conditions prevail, or a disguised restriction on international trade.

Indonesia can legally take measures while promoting free trade. When the Minister of Finance of the Republic of Indonesia enacted No. 137.1/PMK. O11/2014 and applied it, some countries opposed it and brought a WTO suit.

Indonesia and Taiwan (China Taipei) do not have a formal relation or diplomatic office. The only representative relationship between the two countries is the Taiwan Trade Center in Jakarta and the Indonesian Economic and Trade Office of Taipei in Taiwan. Those offices covered ordinary matter when Indonesia had a dispute with Taiwan. But, Indonesia and Vietnam are a member of ASEAN.

ASEAN was founded on August 8, 1967, as a regional organization for the South-East Asian Nation. ASEAN has founded in 5 countries and Indonesia was represented by Indonesia Foreign Minister Adam, the Philippines was represented by Philippines Narcisso Ramos, Malaysia was

151) *Ibid*, Para 7.18, p.15.

represented by Malaysia Vice Minister Tun Abdul Razaq, Singapore was represented by Singapore Foreign Minister S.Rajaratnam and Thailand was represented by Foreign Minister Thanat Khoman that formally create Bangkok Declaration 1967 as a foundation of ASEAN. In 2008 ASEAN created the 2008 ASEAN Charter to strengthen the legal basis of ASEAN status as an International Organization.

The ASEAN has agreed on the establishment of the dispute settlement body in 1996 with official protocol nomenclature. Member used the 1996 Protocol on Dispute Settlement Mechanism and it later was amended to ASEAN Protocol on Enhanced Dispute Settlement Mechanism 2012.

ASEAN has a unique political view of ASEAN, and it is called an ASEAN way. This concept of ASEAN way is implicitly shown in Article 2 verse 2 of ASEAN Charter 2008. According to Article 5 verse 1 of ASEAN Charter 2008, every member of ASEAN has an equal duty and right as a member of ASEAN. There is no country taking a special advantage similar to the United Nation, especially the Security Council. Furthermore, every decision in ASEAN is created under the consensus of all members of ASEAN and it is stated in Article 20 of ASEAN charter.

The dispute settlement system itself is similar to WTO/DSB, but the biggest question is until today there is no official record of DSM ever officially used by ASEAN member country. It is true that all of ASEAN country is indeed WTO member, but ASEAN countries still feel more convinced to use international dispute forum rather than a regional forum.

(2) "In a covered agreement"

Both parties argue that this case relates to the Safeguard Agreement. Also, Indonesia claimed that Panel exceeded its terms of reference by finding a violation of Art I:1 on the measure taken to the galvalume "as a stand-alone measure", i.e. not as a safeguard measure as parties argue. However, the Appellate Body concluded that the description of the specific duty in the complainants' panel requests clearly identified it as a measure alleged to be causing the violation of an obligation contained "in a covered agreement". In this context, Panel simply applied the measure at issue to MFN treatment obligation violation. The Appellate Body found the Panel did not make an error.

In Brazil – Desiccated Coconut, the Appellate Body defined the term "covered agreements" as follows: "The 'covered agreements' include the WTO Agreement, the Agreements in Annexes 1 and 2, as well as any Plurilateral Trade Agreement in Annex 4 where its Committee of signatories has taken a decision to apply the DSU. In a dispute brought to the DSB, a panel may deal with all the relevant provisions of the covered agreements cited by the parties to the dispute in one proceeding[152]. In another case of Guatemala – Cement I, the Appellate Body examined the Panel's interpretation of the relationship between Article 17 of the Anti-Dumping Agreement and the rules and procedures of the DSU. In this context, the Appellate Body made the following general statement about Article 1.1 of the DSU: 1 Appellate Body Report, Brazil – Desiccated Coconut, p. 13. WTO ANALYTICAL INDEX DSU – Article 1/Appendix 1 & 2 (Jurisprudence) 3 "Article 1.1 of the DSU establishes an integrated dispute settlement system which applies to all of the agreements listed in Appendix 1 to the DSU (the 'covered agreements'). The DSU is a coherent system of rules and procedures for dispute settlement which applies to disputes brought pursuant to the consultation and dispute settlement provisions of' the covered agreements. The Anti-Dumping Agreement is a covered agreement listed in Appendix 1 of the DSU; the rules and procedures of the DSU, therefore, apply to disputes brought pursuant to the consultation and dispute settlement provisions contained in Article 17 of that Agreement"[153].

152) Appellate Body Report, Brazil – Desiccated Coconut, p. 13, WTO Analytical Index, DSU-Article 1/Appendix 1& 2, p.2.

153) Appellate Body Report, Guatemala – Cement I, para. 64. WTO Analytical Index, DSU-Article 1/Appendix 1& 2, p.2.

Part III

International Arbitration Cases

10. Churchill Mining PLC v. Indonesia

11. Rafat Ali Rizvi v. Indonesia

III International Arbitration Cases

10. Churchill Mining PLC v. Indonesia

Key Principle: Investment business established with a fabricated signature in the permit process does not deserve protection in International law

1) Facts

Churchill Mining plc. is a British-owned company engaged in mining in Indonesia, where its main activity focus on coal[154]. The company also cooperates with Ridlatama Company in the EKCP project (East Kutai Coal Project) together with the company from Australia Planet Mining pty.Ltd. Churchill announced that they had found a coal reserves around 150 million tons, which will gain a lot of benefit for future[155]. Therefore, Churchill Mining was then interested in investing their capital by acquiring a 75% stake owned by PT. Ridlatama in developing the East Kutai Coal Project (EKCP). In 2007, the Kutai government had issued 4 Mining authority for related companies[156]. Due to the promising project, Churchill asked the East Kutai government to increase the Mining Authority to see an increase in the status of this coal project. Thus, On April 9, 2008, Churchill were then granted an exploration permit for 40 years covering the area of East Kutai Coal Project[157].

Problems arosed on May 4, 2010, due to the East Kutai district

154) See about Churchill Mining bussines on their official website: http://www.churchillmining.com.

155) Fidelia & Syahmin AK, *Analisis Putusan (Award) Arbitrase Internasional ICSID Dalam Churchill Mining Cases Versus Pemerintah Indonesia,* Simbur Cahaya, Fakultas Hukum Universitas Sriwijaya, p.1611.

156) *Ibid.*

157) Aprianto Cahyo, *Churchill Mining Siapkan Gugatan Internasional Terhadap RI,* last modified december 7, 2019, https://ekonomi.bisnis.com/read/20120404/44/71341/churchill-mining-siapkan-gugatan-internasional-terhadap-ri.

government revoked the Mining Business License of PT. Ridlatama Group. The revocation has happened because[158]:

(1) Supreme Audit Board finds that there are indications that Mining Authorization or Mining Business Permit obtained is fabricated;

(2) Mining Authorities obtained by Ridlatama Group are not registered with the East Kutai Regency Planology Mining Service;

(3) In carrying out mining activities in the forest area there was no permit from the Forestry Ministry;

(4) The Ridlatama Company has transferred shares to foreign investors without the Indonesian government's permission and is not in accordance with procedures established by the Indonesian government regarding foreign investment.

Certainly, in response to the decision by Kutai government, Churchill through its subsidiary, PT. Ridlatama which is one of the companies in the Ridlatama group filed a lawsuit through Samarinda Administration Court on August 27, 2010, regarding the Decree of the East Kutai Regent regarding the revocating the business license[159]. The verdict was read on March 3, 2011, which essentially rejected the plaintiff's lawsuit. It said that the district head of East Kutai did not violated the procedure when it made a decision to revoke his business permit.[160] Not satisfied with this decision, Churchill applied to the Administrative High Court and the court upheld the Samarinda Administrative Court decision. In 2011, Churchill also submitted Judicial Review to the Supreme Court of the Republic of Indonesia, but his appeal was rejected again.

158) Yuni Ayu Sitanggang, "Upaya Churchill Mining Plc Dalam Penyelesaian Sengketa Dengan Pemerintah Kutai Timur Terkait Pencabutan Izin PT. Ridlatama", *EJournal Hubungan Internasional* Vol. 2 No.4, p.942.

159) Michael Allan, *Churchill Mining's $2-billion lawsuit will not be heard by Indonesia's Supreme Court,* last modified december 7, 2019, https://archive.ph/20130103223732/http://www.mining.com/2012/06/14/indonesias-supreme-court-rejects-churchill-minings-appeal#selection-973.0-973.84.

160) *Ibid.*

Finally, Churchill brought this dispute to the International Center for Settlement of Investment Dispute (ICSID) arbitration body. ICSID is an international arbitration institution established in 1966 for legal dispute resolution and conciliation between international investors. ICSID is an independent, depoliticized and effective dispute-settlement institution. Its availability to investors and States helps to promote international investment by providing confidence in the dispute resolution process. The plaintiffs (Churchill Mining Plc and Planet Mining Pty Ltd) registered their claim in the ICSID international arbitration forum with Case Number ARB / 12/14 and 12/40 which were registered by the Plaintiffs on 22 June 2012 and 26 December 2012 to the ICSID forum based on the bilateral investment treaty (BIT) Indonesia – United Kingdom and Indonesia – Australlia.

Churchill brought this case based on violations, namely indirect expropriation, which is a form of nationalization accompanied by payment of compensation. Furthermore, other allegations are related to the principle of fair and equitable treatment through revocation of Mining Authorization / Exploitation Mining Business Permit[161]. The claimant brought are as follows[162]:

(1) The respondent (Republic of Indonesia) has violated its international obligations under the BIT Agreement;

(2) Order the respondent to pay full compensation in accordance with the BIT Agreement and international customary law, the amount of which will be determined further by arbitration;

(3) Order the respondent to pay all arbitration fees, including but not

161) Kementrian Hukum dan Hak Asasi Manusia Republik Indonesia, *Indonesia Raih Kemenangan Mutlak di Forum Arbitrase ICSID,* last modified December 6, 2019, https://kemenkumham.go.id/berita/indonesia -raih-kemenangan-mutlak-di-forum-arbitrase-icsid.

162) Huala Adolf, "Sengketa Penanaman Modal antara Investor Melawan Pemerintah Indonesia di Arbitrase ICSID", *Padjajaran Jurnal Ilmu Hukum*, Vol.1 No.3, p.437.

limited to the costs and fees of the Arbitral Tribunal and legal service fees;

(4) Order the respondent to pay interest as long as the ruling has not been carried out in the amount according to the appropriate arbitration body; and

(5) Order other actions that the Arbitration Tribunal deems appropriate.

Furthermore, the Plaintiffs claimed that the violation had caused losses to its investment in Indonesia, and filed a lawsuit amounting to USD 1.3 billion (approximately IDR 18 Trillion).

2) Court Decision

The Indonesian government argued that the ICSID Arbitration Council did not have a legal basis to handle this dispute, because there was no legal basis for the Indonesian government to submit a dispute with Churchill and Planet to the ICSID arbitration body.

On February 24, 2014, the ICSID Tribunal Assembly issued a ruling that ICSID was authorized to examine and adjudicate the arbitration lawsuit and other things such as indications of falsification of documents by the plaintiffs would be on the agenda at the hearing of the principal case. The legal basis used by the assembly is the negotiating record (negotiation *or travaux préparatoire)* regarding the articles of the agreement. In the trial, the applicant pointed out that the word intended during the negotiation was or in line with the definition of "hereby consent"[163)].

On September 24, 2014, the Government of Indonesia submitted an application to the ICSID Tribunal Assembly to stop the entire arbitration

163) *Ibid,* ICSID, *Churcill Mining Plc v. Indonesia Decision on Jurisdiction,* 24 February 2014, Para.310-319.

process (Request for Dismissal) based on fake or forgery mining permit documents. The Indonesian government also requested the ICSID Tribunal Assembly to examine the alleged forgery first before entering into the subject matter. In November 2014, the ICSID Tribunal Assembly accepted Indonesia's view and decided to examine the document forgery issue first before entering into the subject matter.

On December 6, 2016, the Tribunal consisting of Professor Gabrielle Kaufmann-Kohler, Michael Hwang SC, and Professor Albert Jan van den Berg ("ICSID Tribunal") rejected all claims filed by the Plaintiffs against the Republic of Indonesia. The ICSID Tribunal subsequently granted the Indonesian Government's claim to receive an award on costs of USD 9.4 Million[164].

In the course of the trial which was later confirmed in its decision, the ICSID Tribunal accepted arguments and evidence, including forensic expert statements submitted by the Indonesian government to prove the existence of duplication, which indicating the use of an autopen machine. There were 34 fake documents submitted by the Plaintiffs in the trial (including mining permits for the general survey and exploration stage) which seemed to be official / original documents issued by various government agencies in Indonesia, both central and regional. The ICSID Tribunal agreed with the Indonesian government's argument that "investments that are against the law do not deserve protection in international law." ICSID further mentioned that "The Plaintiffs did not carry out their obligations to examine their local work partners and supervise their licensing processes (lack of diligence)." Therefore, based on the facts and considerations as stated, the ICSID Tribunal stated that the claims of the Plaintiffs were rejected[165].

Plaintiffs also submitted an application for annulment of the award. The

164) ICSID, Churcill v. Indonesia Award, December 06, 2016.
165) Kementrian Hukum dan Hak Asasi Manusia Republik Indonesia, *Op.Cit.*.

arguments submitted by the Plaintiffs are as follows:

(1) The ICSID Tribunal is deemed to have overstepped the authority (*ultra vires*);

(2) There has been a serious deviation from the basic rules of procedure;

(3) The decision has failed to state the reasons on which the decision was based.

Finally, through a long struggle, on 18 March 2019 the ICSID Committee reaffirmed Indonesia's victory through a final ruling and permanent legal force (Decision on Annulment).

3) Comments

(1) Jurisdiction

ICSID jurisdiction matters are covered in ICSID Art. 25-27 of ICSID Convention. The issue brought by Indonesia in this dispute is the jurisdiction. The Tribunal believes that under the ICSID Convention, an agreement to submit a dispute to ICSID arbitration must be stated in writing. Apart from these conditions, there are no other conditions, such as "the provision of the agreement must be clear and unambiguous". In this dispute, the Panel also reviewed the Vienna Convention on the Law Treaties Article 31 and 32 regarding the interpretation of an agreement. In this decision, ICSID rejected the Indonesian government's claim stating that ICSID has no jurisdiction. It is true that the approval given by BKPM to a company does not contain approval of dispute resolution at the ICSID.

In this case, tribunal believed that the BKPM[166)] had informed president about ICSID resolution method since the BKPM is as an important institution that is directly responsible to the president. If the BKPM have

166) BKPM or Indonesian Investment Coordinating Board is a Non-Ministerial Government Agency, which in charge of implementing policy and service coordination in investment in accordance with the provisions of the regulations.

exceeded their authority, then the president would have intervened.

(2) Forgery of Document

In this case, a very important fact brought by Indonesia is the legal basis for issuing the revocation of mining exploration licenses to Churcill as well as 34 falisificated signatures. ICSID discussed the legality of the documents in the permit decision before discussing the main issues raised by the plaintiff is also a concern of ICSID. In its decision, ICISD said that "investments that are against the law do not deserve protection in international law" and "The Plaintiffs did not carry out their obligations to examine their local work partners and supervise their licensing processes (lack of diligence)".

11. Rafat Ali Rizvi v. Indonesia

Key Principle: Fulfilling permit and approval requirement stated under domestic regulation as well as BIT is precondition to ICSID dispute

1) Facts

This case concern Rafat Ali Rizki, a British citizen. He filed a dispute in ICSID against Indonesian government on May 19, 2011. Rafat Ali appointed Joan Donaghue (US citizen) as the arbitrator of his choice. The Indonesian government appointed Prof. Mutchucumaraswamy Sornarajah (Australian citizen). Both parties agreed to appoint Prof. Gavan Griffith (Australian) as chair of the Arbitration Tribunal.

The power of government representatives was represented by the Attorney General's Office. This case began when Mr. Rafat invested in Indonesia through a company called Chinkara Capital Limited. Chinkara acquired Century Bank and Rafat was one of the major shareholders of Chinkara Ltd[167].

On November 21, 2008 Century Bank became a failed bank that had an impact to the Indonesian economy. Thus, Indonesian government issued a policy with Bailout funds in the amount of IDR 6.700.000.000 (6.7 Trilion Rupiah)[168]. As the result of this policy, Mr. Rafat felt injured and sued Indonesian government for issuing the Bailout policy. He sued Indonesian government to pay compensation in the amount of USD 75 Million[169]. The legal basis that he used was the Bilateral Investment Treaty ("BIT") between Indonesia and United Kingdom and the Law No. 1/1967 on the

167) International Centre For Settlement Of Investment Disputes Washington, D.C., *Award On Jurisdiction*, ICSID Case No. ARB/11/13, Rafat Ali Rizvi v. Indonesia, July 16, 2013.
168) Huala Adolf, *Op.Cit*, p.442.
169) Idik Saeful Bahri, *Pembahasan Kasus Investasi Rafat Ali Rizvi,* last modified march 12, 2020. https://www.researchgate.net/publication/339165352_Pembahasan_Kasus_Investasi_Rafat_Ali_Rizvi.

protection of Foreign Investment.

However, Indonesian government raised objection to the ICSID regarding the jurisdiction of the case. According to Indonesian government, the investment done by Mr. Rafat is considered as the Foreign Portofolio Investment or indirect investment, under BIT according to No.1/1967. The purchase of shares carried out by Mr. Rafat was through the stock exchange and direct stock purchase. The Indonesian investment provisions requires the establishment of a foreign investment company to be processed through the Investment Coordinating Board[170).

The plaintiff (Mr. Rafat) opposed that argument saying that the Foreign Investment Law of Indonesia Art. 5 allows a flexibility and the foreign investment can be done through other body besides the Investment Coordinating Board. And he also argued that the Art. 1 of BIT regarding the investment is not limited to the direct investment.

2) Court Decision

Aricle 25 verse 1 of ICSID Convention states that the jurisdiction must fulfill below elements, which are:[171)]

(1) There must be a legal dispute;
(2) There are legal disputes that arise directly from the transaction in dispute; and
(3) The Parties to the dispute need to consent in writing to submit the suit to ICSID

170) Ricky & Yu Un, *Kualifikasi Penanaman Modal Oleh Icsid Sebagai Forum Penyelesaian Sengketa Penanaman Modal Asing (Studi Kasus: Icsid Award On Jurisdiction No. Arb/11/13 Dalam Perkara Antara Rafat Ali Rizvi Melawan Republik Indonesia)*, Fakultas Hukum Universitas Indonesia, p.2.

171) ICSID Convention, Regulations and Rules. Washington, D.C.: International Centre for Settlement of Investment Disputes, 2003. Art. 25.

The tribunal also mentioned that there must be 3 cumulative elements that must be fulfilled by the plaintiff under the present case, in which[172]:

(1) Investments;

(2) By nationals or companies of the United Kingdom; and

(3) In the territory of the Republic of Indonesia.

Since Mr. Rafat has invested in Centry Bank, it really is clear that on the first element the plaintiff didn't fulfill, because actually the one who invested in Century Bank was Chinkara, not the Plaintiff himself. So, the investment elements were not fulfilled, because there was no investment made by the Plaintiff at Century Bank[173].

Therefore, under the present case, the tribunal concluded that[174]his status of shareholder does not fulfill the requirement under the BIT.

(1) Accept objection of the Respondent on the jurisdiction matter that the Petitioner's investment is not granted with a permit required under the Indonesian Foreign Investment Capital Law as welll as BIT Article 2(1). , Therefore, it is not within the scope of the BIT;

(2) Refuse the Applicant's dependence on the MFN provisions from BIT since this case is not applicable to questions about the scope of the BIT in the circumstances;

(3) State that the Center and the Court do not have jurisdiction over this dispute; and

(4) Make an order for costs to allocate costs between the Parties together with each party bearing its own costs and legal representation.

---

172) Agreement between the Government of the United Kingdom of Great Britain and Northern Ireland and the Government of the Republic of Indonesia for the Promotion and Protection of Investments 1976 [Hereinafter as Bilateral Investement Agreement] Art. 2 verse 1.

173) Ricky, *Op.cit,* p.2.

174) International Centre For Settlement Of Investment Disputes Washington, D.C., *Award On Jurisdiction*, ICSID Case No. ARB/11/13, Rafat Ali Rizvi v. Indonesia, July 16, 2013.

3) Comments

(1) Indirect Investment

Both BIT and Indonesian Foreign Investment Law requires permit of the Investment Coordinating Body. Investment conducted by Rafat Ali falls under the definition of indirect Foreign Investment. It is clear that the Foreign Direct Investment that being protected under the BIT must be through permission of Investment Coordinating Body of Indonesia. Investments made by Rafat Ali on Century Bank shares are investments made through third parties, the Chinkara Limited. which domiciled in the Bahamas. Thus, this is not included within the scope of BIT Agreement.

Because Rafat Ali's Investment in Century Bank shares is not included in the scope of investment in the Indonesian and British PMPA and BIT Laws, the ICSID arbitration institution is not authorized to examine and decide upon the application filed by Rafat Ali[175].

Most of foreign investors tend to bring or threaten the Indonesian government to the ICSID forum when foreign parties feel disadvantaged investment conditions in Indonesia. In this case, Indonesian government have acted in accordance with the applicable laws. This decision reaffirms permit or approval from BKPM is an absolute requirement for an investment to get legal protection[176].

175) Idik, *Op.cit,* p.5-6.
176) Huala Adolf, *Op.cit,* p.444.

Part IV

Treaty Case

12. ASEAN Charter-Constitutional Court Case

IV Treaty Case

12. ASEAN Charter-Constitutional Court Case[177)]

Key Principle: The internal mechanism adopted by each country for implementation is different from the mechanism given at the Vienna Convention on the law of treaties

1) Facts

In 2011, a group of NGOs and individuals petitioned for a Judicial Review of Law No.38 of 2008 for the unconstitutionality. Those NGOs are Non-Government Organization Global Justice Institute Association, INFID Association, Aliansi Petani Indonesia (API)[178)], Serikat Petani Indonesia (SPI)[179)], Perkumpulan Koalisi Rakyat Untuk Keadilan Perikanan (KIARA)[180)], National Front of the Indonesian Workers'Struggle (FNPBI), Indonesian Association for Sovereign Migrant Workers (Migrant Care), Associates for Small Business Women (ASSPPUK). Three individuals also joined the petition. Law No. 38/2008 is implemented for the purpose of ratification of the ASEAN Charter. This Law No. 38/2008 purposed that 'single market and production base' with 'free flow of goods, services and investment' and 'free flow of capital'. The Constitutional court handed down the decision on 4th February 2013.

2) Court Decision

Plaintiff claimed that "Law No. 38 of 2008 has been the legal basis for the entrance of a trade agreement"[181)]. Plaintiff also claimed that the

177) Decision of Constitutional Court, ASEAN Charter Case 33/PUU-IX/2011.
178) Indonesian Farmers Alliance.
179) Indonesian Farmers Association.
180) People Coalition Association for Fishery Justice.
181) ASEAN Charter Case, p.58.

enforcement of FTAs, following affiliation to ASEAN (Association of Southeast Asian Nations) such as ASEAN-China[182], ASEAN-India[183], ASEAN-Australia-New Zealand[184], ASEAN-Japan[185], made Indonesian companies lose competitiveness of national products. When companies went bankrupt then workers lost their jobs[186] Plaintiff argued that "the pro-market policies advocated in the ASEAN Charter sought the opposite policy of market-sovereignty"[187]. Plaintiff also argued that "Implementation of the Law No. 38/2008 has broken the pillar of economic, social-cultural fundamental that Article 27(2) and Article 33 of the 1945 Indonesian Constitution have stated"[188][189].

The government first argued that the Constitutional Court was not authorized to test ratification of the international agreement. ASEAN Charter was declared valid on December 15, 2008, following the own rule of procedure which is different from the ratification process stated in the 1945 Constitution of Indonesia[190]or Law No.38/2008.

182) Ratified by the Presidential Decree No. 48 of 2004.
183) Presidential Decree No. 69 of 2004.
184) Presidential Regulation No. 26 of 2011.
185) Presidential Regulation No. 50 of 2009.
186) ASEAN Charter Case p.58.
187) *Ibid.*, p.66.
188) The hierarchy of the Indonesian law is stated in Article 7 of Law No.20 of 2011 concerning Making Rule. The order follows 1. 1945 Constitution of the Republic of Indonesia 2. People's Consultative Council Decree 3. Law/Government Regulation *in Lieu of Law*, Government Regulation 4. Presidential Regulation 5. Province Regulation 6. Regency/Municipality Regulation.
189) ASEAN Charter Case, pp.66~73.
190) *Ibid.*

Section X: Citizens and Residents
Article 27

1. All citizens shall have equal status before the law and the government and hold without exemption the law and the government in esteem.

2. Each citizen shall be entitled to an occupation and an existence proper for a human being.

3. Each citizen shall have the right and the duty to participate in the defense of the nation.

Section XIV: National Economy and Social Welfare
Article 33

1.The economy is to be structured as a common endeavor based on familial principles.

Production sectors that are vital to the state and that affect the livelihood of a considerable part of the population are to be controlled by the state.

The land and the waters as well as the natural riches therein are to be controlled by the state to be exploited to the greatest benefit of the people.

The organization of the national economy shall be based on economic democracy that upholds the principles of solidarity, efficiency along with fairness, sustainability, keeping the environment in perspective, self-sufficiency, and that is concerned as well with balanced progress and with the unity of the national economy.

Further provisions regarding the implementation of this article are to be regulated by law.

The government also argued that the normative material of the ASEAN Charter was not included in Law No. 38/2008. The approval of the House of Representatives (Dewan Perwakilan Rakyat: hereafter DPR) does not have a dual function of ratification through the law as well as the transformation of provisions of the international agreement. The practice of Indonesia is "new international agreement can be implemented effectively at the national level after being transformed into statutory regulations of the nation itself"[191]. Having said that, the government responded to the claim of the plaintiff that the implementation of free trade agreement has taken into account the sovereignty of each country, so the principle of kindship as referred to in Article 33 of the 1945 Constitution is also reflected in ASEAN. Besides, the government stands to the reason that Article 33 does not prohibit competition among business actors as long as the competition does not negate control by the state which includes the power to regulate, manage and supervise[192]. In addition to that, Law No. 7/2014 on trade provides that treaties directed toward enhancing Indonesian market access must be approved by the legislature. Since this kind of protective measure is embedded in the system, the government argued that the principle of kindship was properly enforced.

Constitutional Court concluded that the Constitutional Court had the authority to adjudicate petition[193] since the Constitutional Court held the first and final level for its decision when testing the Constitutionality of the norms of the Act[194]. In the reasoning, eight judges (with two dissenting judges) out of ten denied the argument of the government saying that Law No. 38/2008 served as a legal basis of the validity of the ASEAN Charter in Indonesia, therefore the Charter was an integrated part of Indonesian law[195].

The Court said the use of approval of the DPR has only an external binding legal force against other countries. Different mechanisms are needed from an internal point to confirm the consent of binding DPR's approval of the international agreement. The Internal mechanism adopted by each country is different from the mechanism given at the Vienna

191) *Ibid.*, p.96.
192) *Ibid.*, p.156.
193) *Ibid.*, p.181.
194) *Ibid.*
195) *Ibid.*, pp. 199~204. Rina Shahriyani Sharulla, Park, Jihyun "Implementation of International Treaty in Indonesia and Adoption of the Indonesian Court", *Yonsei Law Review*, Vol. 28. No.1, March 2018. p.317; Dr. jur. Damos Dumoli Agusman, "Treaties under Indonesian Law", PT Remaja Rosdakarya, 2014, p.383.

Convention on the Law of Treaties[196]. ASEAN Charter required the ratification method to be taken by the participating countries[197].

Constitutional Court pointed out that "the government holds the obligation to respect the principle of *Pacta Sunt Servanda*[198]". At the same time, "the Indonesian government in making the implementation rules must be in accordance with interests in the 1945 Constitution[199]" The ASEAN charter states at the Art. 5(2) that 'Member States shall take all necessary measures, including the enactment of appropriate domestic legislation, to effectively implement the provisions of this Charter and to comply with all obligations of membership'.

3) Comments

(1) Monism, Dualism

This ASEAN Charter case has a big implication on the issue of treaty implementation[200]. Academia of Indonesia shows the mixed opinion of Monism, Dualism on the issue of Indonesian practice of implementation of a treaty to domestic law. Dualism practice dominates in court practice in the field of private law. But monism practice is also found in the court practice. Before an enactment of the Indonesian Treaty Law, president letter No 2826/HK/1960 played a role of subjective and procedure matter of the treaty conclusion. This letter differentiates 'treaty (in Bahasa: perjanjian)' and 'agreement (in Bahasa: persetujuan)' and only important matters such as political matters are processed as treaty[201] with

196) *Ibid.*, pp. 194~196.
197) The ASEAN Charter Art. 47.
198) The ASEAN Charter case *Ibid.*, p.180.
199) *Ibid.*,p.196.
200) For the matter of treaty implementation, refer to Eddy Pratomo, Hukum Perjanjian Internasional, Pengertian Status Hukum dan Ratifikasi. Penerbit Alumni, Bandung 2011.
201) i) Political matters or other matters that could affect foreign policy, such as treaties of friendship, treaties of alliance, treaties with the effect of changing territories or boundary treaties ii) Binding relationships that might affect foreign policy iii) Matters that in accordance with the Constitution or the Law, such as nationality and justice administration, should be regulated by laws.

approval of DPR[202]. In 2000, Law No. 24/2000 on Treaties has finally been enacted. However, still, this does not clear the ambiguity on the practice of Indonesian treaty implementation. One thing is clear that the absence of domestic law cannot be an excuse for breaching International law from the perspective of International law[203].

Article 4 of the Indonesian Treaty Law stipulates the obligation of good faith and consideration of the national interest when the government concludes treaties with other parties. Art. 9 of the law reads "ratification of a treaty by the Government of the Republic of Indonesia shall be conducted provided it is required by the treaty". Then Art. 10 enlists the subject matters that require parliamentary approval. Those are 1) political issues, peace, defense and state security 2) Territorial changes or establishing state boundaries 3) Sovereignty or sovereign rights 4) Human rights and environment 5) Formation of new legal norms 6) Loan and grant-aid agreements.

Art. 11 then states that "(1) ratification of a treaty, the material of which is not stipulated in Art.10 done by a presidential decree. (2) The Government of the Republic of Indonesia submits a copy of the presidential decree ratifying the treaty to the House of Representatives for evaluation". This current disparity of Art. 10 and 11 of the treaty law and Art. 11 of the constitution[204] also generates ambiguity and dual practice by a government entity.

The monistic state adopts the doctrine of incorporation or adoption. The direct applicability and/or direct effect (domestic effect) of each treaty differs depending on each state. Indonesia does not allow direct applicability nor direct effect in the court except for some human rights

202) However, the loan agreement between Indonesia and the Netherland on 1 March 1951 passed the parliamentary approval through Law No. 4 of 1951.

203) The Alabama Claims Arbitration of 1987.

204) Article 11 states (1)President with the approval of People's Representative Council declares war, make peace, and agreement with other countries.; (2) President, in making other Treaty that result in a wide and profound impact on social life related with the state's financial burden, and/or obliges change or drafting Constitution, must with the approval of People's Representative Council;(3) Further requirement on Treaty is regulated by Laws".

convention. In such a situation, the Constitutional Court went with the logic of the ASEAN Charter as well as the practice of Indonesia concluding that the treaty cannot be applied without domestic legislation. 1990 case of the U.N. Convention on the Recognition and Enforcement of Foreign Arbitral Awards[205]is clear evidence of the non-applicability of the ratified treaty. This Convention is ratified through the Keputusan Presiden No. 34 Tahun 1981 but it was possible to apply it after the legislation of Peraturan Mahkamah Agung Republik Indonesia No. 1/1990[206]. Recent No. 13/PUU-XVI/2018 decision also emphasizes that "ratification is one way to declare to be bound by a treaty" and the ratification process in this context only has an effect on members of the treaty[207].

(2) Self-Executing Treaty

Self-executing treaties do not have an effect in Indonesia since the Indonesian judicial body requires individuals to provide a cause of action from the domestic law in the Indonesian court. Treaty may be used as customary International law by Indonesian judges to make decisions when they handle cases relating to a treaty as a part of evidence but not as the sole ground of the decision. The plaintiff may also quote convention as a piece of evidence. The International community sees Indonesia's practice concerning the treaty as a form of adoption through customary international law. In the case concerning Sovereignty over Pulau Ligitan and Pulau Sipadan, 2002,[208] the ICJ stated that 'through Article 31 and 32 of the Vienna Convention, Indonesia subscribe to the provisions of the

205) 330 U.N.T.S.38. signed on 10th June 1958. Enforced on 7th June 1959.

206) Supreme Court Decision, case No. 2944 K/Pdt/1983. See: E. Rajagukguk, Arbitrase dalam Putusan Pengadilan,, Jakarta, 2001, pp. 284-288.

207) The ASEAN Charter case, *Ibid.*,p.195.

208) D.D. Agusman, *Treaties Under Indonesian Law: A Comparative Study (*Bandung, 2014), p. 21; List of international treaties that Indonesia has ratified/acceded to that is maintained by the Ministry of Foreign Affairs is available at http://treaty.kemlu.go.id/index.php/treaty/index.

Convention by virtue of customary international law'.[209)]

The self-executing treaty concept is found as early as 1909 Maiorano v. B. & O. P.R.R. Co. case in the U.S[210)]. At that time, the court explains "A treaty ...by the express words of the Constitution, is the supreme law of the land, binding alike National and State Courts, and is capable of enforcement, and must be enforced by them in the ligation of private rights." The term "self-executing" was a bit cleared in the case of Medellin v. Texas, 2008 552 U.S. (2008). Chief justice Robert explained it as below.

"what we mean by "self-executing" is that the treaty has an automatic domestic effect as federal law upon ratification. Conversely, a "non-self-executing" treaty does not by itself give rise to domestically enforceable federal law. Where such a treaty has domestic effect depends upon implementing legislation passed by Congress. Even when treaties are self-executing in the sense that they create federal law, the background presumption is that "international agreements, even those directly benefiting private persons, generally do not create private rights or provide for a private cause of action in domestic court".

Since self-executing provisions and non-self-executing provisions are mixed in one treaty, deciding the character of the provision will be the first issue to solve when there is an issue relating to monism or dualism.

(3) Why Re-Negotiating of The Treaty Provision is Possible? -Separability of Treaty Provisions (Vienna Convention Art. 44)[211)]

209) *Ibid.*, p.233.

210) Foster and Elam v. Neilson 27 U.S.(2 Pet.) 253 (1829) case, Judge Marshall differentiated the self-executing treaty by saying that "A treaty is in its nature a contract between two nations, not a legislative act. It does not generally affect, of itself, the object to be accomplished, especially so far as its operation is infra-territorial: but is carried into execution by the sovereign power of the respective parties to the instrument....Our Constitution declares a treaty to be the law of the land...But when the terms of the stipulation import a contract...and the legislature must execute the contract before it can become a rule for the court." Daeson Kim, "International law", Samyoungsa, 17th ed. P. 287 footnote 172.

211) Detailed explanation on the Art. 44 of the Vienna Treaty was covered at Park Jihyun, "Study

The severance of provisions in the treaty has long been discussed by the academia. However, their opinions were swayed by judicial decisions. Traditionally, legal experts opinioned that the integrity of the treaty is such an important factor, and this element cannot be broken. Every provision is interdependent and inseparable, the whole treaty is overall compact which cannot be broken down even non-essential provisions cannot be separated. However, along with the heterogeneous perspective of bilateral treaties, the change of the view on the 'integrity' of the treaty came.

Now, the separability of a treaty is accepted both by the academia and judicial arena. Article 44 of the Vienna Convention on the Treaties cover invalidating, terminating, withdrawing, suspending of the clauses(provision).

In the Free zones case, ICJ concluded that Article 435 of the Treaty of Versailles and Annex was a "complete whole" independent of the rest of the Treaty[212)]. Also, In the S.S. Wimbledon case, section VI part XII of the treaty is considered "self-contained"[213)]. In the case of Certain Norwegian Loans[214)], ICJ upheld that Norwegian's preliminary objection base on the principle of reciprocity on the issue of the ICJ's jurisdiction to hear this case due to the reservation on the ICJ Art.36(2) made by France. Lauterpacht, in his separate opinion, stated that only invalid provision among the whole treaty can be deemed null[215)]. He stated back in 1933 "The rule that compacts must be kept is certainly one of the bases of the legal relations between the members of any community. But at the same time, the notion that in certain cases the law will refuse to continue to give effect

on the Vienna Convention Art. 44, Separability of treaty provisions", *Korea International Law Review*, Vol.53, 2019.6.30, pp. 9-28.

212) Case of the Free Zones of Upper Savoy and the District of Gex, (Switzerland v. France), 1929 PCIJ, Series A, No.22.

213) S.S. 'Wimbledon' (France v. Germany), Judgement of 17 August 1923, PCIJ, Series A, No. 1, p.24.

214) Case of Certain Norwegian Loans (France v. Norway), Judgement, I.C.J. Reports 1957, p.9.

215) Separate Opinion of Judge Lauterpacht in Certain Norwegian Loans, Judgement of 6 July 1956, ICJ Reports 1956, pp. 56-7.

to originally valid contracts is common to all systems of jurisprudence"[216].

The distinction between essential and non-essential clauses is also mentioned in the Fisheries Jurisdiction case[217]. The ICJ noted that the ability of the applicants to have recourse to the ICJ in the case of unilateral extension of exclusive fisheries jurisdiction into the sea by Iceland was an essential element of the conventional *quid pro quo*[218]. In a separate opinion of the case South West Africa, Judge Jessup, Spender, and Fitzmaurice explore the opinion on the separability of the 'non-essential' provision of the treaty[219]. Of course, the opinion of the case of the Reservations to the Genocide Conventions[220] shows the line that essential part of the treaty and not-essential part of the treaty in question. In the Genocide case, ICJ came up with the historical statement that the compatibility of a reservation with the object and purpose of the treaty is the criterion to determine the permissibility of reservations and objections thereto[221].

Academically, the 1935 Harvard Research Draft mentioned that 1912 Règlement concernant *les effets de la guerre'* (Regulations on the effects of the outbreak of war) rules of severance when the provision has different nature. 1963 draft of Foreign Relations Law of the United States from the American Law Institute supported the separability of the treaty.

"*Utile non devet per inutile vitiari*" that McNair has cited means "That which is useful or valid ought not to be vitiated by that which is superfluous or invalid." This proverb represents Article 44 of the Vienna Convention of the Treaties.

216) See H. Lauterpacht, The Function of Law in the International Community (Oxford: At the Clarendon Press, 1933), p. 273.

217) Fisheries Jurisdiction(United Kingdom v. Iceland), 25 July 1974, ICJ Reports(1974), pp. 54-5 "The compromissory clause was no mere severable clause of minor significance but an essential element of the entire agreement'.

218) Fisheries Jurisdiction(United Kingdom v. Iceland), 2 February 1973, ICJ Reports(1973), p.13.

219) Separate Opinion of Judge Jessup, and Dissenting Opinions of Judge Spender and Fitzmaurice in the South West Africa cases, Preliminary Objections, Judgement of 21 December 1962, ICJ Reports 1962, pp. 408, 517, and 518.

220) Reservations to the Genocide Convention, Advisory Opinion, ICJ Reports (1951).

221) 1951 Advisory Opinion (Reservations to the Genocide Convention) at p. 24.

Part V

Intellectual Property Rights Cases

13. Indonesia Traditional Herbal in Japan Patent Applied by Shiseido Corp.Ltd.
14. Toyota Motor Corp v. Nio Teddy Siswanto
15. DC Comics, Inc v. PT. Marxing Fam Makmur
16. HUGO BOSS v. Teddy Tan & Alexander
17. Inter IKEA System B.V v. PT. Ratania Khatulistiwa
18. John Hardy Jewelry & PT.Karya Tangan Indah v. Ketut Deni Aryasa
19. Indonesia Monkey Selfie Dispute

V Intellectual Property Rights Cases

13. Indonesia -Japan Co. (Traditional Knowledge & Shiseido Corp. Ltd. Case)

Key Principle: Fair and equitable use of biological diversity, as well as access and benefit-sharing are set rules for the traditional knowledge

1) Facts

The Shiseido Corporation Ltd. is now a multinational cosmetic company starting as Japan's first private western-style pharmacy in Ginza, Tokyo in 1872 advancing into the cosmetics industry in 1897. In 1999, Shesiedo Corp. applied for the patent containing Indonesian traditional herbal substances[222) relating to an anti-aging agent and hair tonic with long pepper (in Bahasa: cube jawa), false daisy (in Bahasa: orang aring), java olive (in Bahasa: jangkang), meniran (*phyllanthuss nirur*) weeping paperback (in Bahasa: merica bolong) chinese finger-root (in Bahasa: temu kunci), bitter ginger (in Bahasa: lempuyang/ *Zingiber Zrumbet*), bitter ginger (in Bahasa: jamu), in Bahasa: Kayu Rapet (*parameria Lavigata*), Kemukus (*Piper cubeba*), Tempuyang (*Sonchus Arvensis*), Belantas (*Pluchea Indica L*), Mesoyi (*Massoia Aromatic Becc*), Pule (*Alstonia Scholaris*), Pulowaras (*Alycai Reindwartiss*), Sintok (Cinnamoumumsintoc BI), Kayu legi (*Glycyrrhiza gloabra*), Kelabet (*Trigonella foenum-graceum*), Remujung (*Orthosiphon Staminens*), Brotowali (*Tinospora Crispa*), etc[223)].

Shiseido applied for patents in 1999 in the Japanese Patent Office under the serial number WO09963905A1, JP10029924A, JP09169628A, JP09169627A, JP09071522A, JP10316541 etc. But soon confronted by the

222) Hank Ten Have, *Global Bioethics: An Introduction*, Routledge, 2016. p.116.
223) Ani Mardiastuti, "Implementation of Access and Benefit Sharing in Indonesia: Review and Case Studies", *Jurnal Managemen Hutan Tropika*, Vol. 25 No.2, April 2019, pp.35-43.

objection and massive boycott against Shiseido by the Indonesian NGO end up withdrawing it.

2) Patent Office

Shiseido Corp. withdrew the patent application containing the Indonesian herb in March 2002.

3) Comments

(1) Culture and Traditional Knowledge

2003 Convention for the Safeguarding of the Intangible Cultural Heritage stipulates the definition of "intangible cultural heritage". It says the practices, representations, expressions, knowledge, skills – as well as the instruments, objects, artifacts and cultural spaces associated therewith – that communities, groups and, in some cases, individuals recognize as part of their cultural heritage. This intangible cultural heritage, transmitted from generation to generation, is constantly recreated by communities and groups in response to their environment, their interaction with nature and their history, and provides them with a sense of identity and continuity, thus promoting respect for cultural diversity and human creativity. For the purposes of this Convention, consideration is given solely to such intangible cultural heritage as is compatible with existing international human rights instruments, as well as with the requirements of mutual respect among communities, groups and individuals, and of sustainable development(Art. 2(1)).

At Art. 2(2), the convention also provides a positive list of domains as (a) oral traditions and expressions, including language as a vehicle of the intangible cultural heritage; (b) performing arts; (c) social practices, rituals and festive events; (d) knowledge and practices concerning nature and the universe; (e) traditional craftsmanship.

Similarly, the definition of "cultural diversity" at the Convention on the Protection and Promotion of the Diversity of Cultural Expression (Cultural Diversity Convention) refers to the manifold ways in which the cultures of groups and societies find expression. These expressions are passed on within and among groups and societies. Cultural diversity is made manifest not only through the varied ways in which the cultural heritage of cultural expression, but also through diverse modes of artistic creation, production, dissemination, distribution and enjoyment, whatever the means and technologies used.

The scope of culture defined in the two agreements is a bit different. Cultural diversity agreement is more aggressively protecting the ongoing process of the formation of culture itself. Providing legal protection to culture seems indefinite and socially acceptable means of protection vary depending on the society. The protection of traditional knowledge or genetic resources also varies. Not only typical protection through IP rights or economic regulations such as Patent, Design, Trademark, GI, Copyright, Unfair Competition, Trade Secret, but also a quality certification of food using traditional process method designated of intangible & tangible cultural heritage, etc. exist. In addition to these, many states have a sui generis system of their own. The conflicting interest of TRIPS 27(3)(b) and sui generis or state protection system is still an ongoing issue in 2020.

So far, the clear part is that the current internationally agreed intellectual property protection system covers only the innovation based on culture (which includes traditional knowledge).

(2) Access and Benefit Sharing

Bioprospecting contract requirements such as prior informed consent and compensation are set at Convention on Biological Diversity (hereafter CBD). At the same time, CBD also encourages the sharing of information.

The fair/equitable sharing of benefits from the genetic resource uses becomes the rule of research as well as means of environmentally sound use.

Cases of the rosy periwinkle[224], the neem tree[225] the Enola bean[226], the Basmati rice[227], the Maya ICBG controversy[228], pushed several countries to digitalize traditional knowledge database in the form of electronic resources providing a link to search in many countries' patent & trademark offices.

Indonesia accepted international treaty Nagoya protocol by Law No.11/2013 on ratification of the Nagoya Protocol on access to genetic resources and the fair and equitable sharing of benefits arising from their utilization to the convention of biological diversity. Draft Law (RUU) of management of genetic resources (PSDG) was introduced in 2005-2009, 2010-2014, 2015-2019 parliament session, but not passed the plenary session. Revision of Law No. 5/1990 on the conservation of biological resources and their ecosystems is currently also a bill. In 2019, It has a new title called "preservation and utilization of genetic resource". Since Indonesia covers biodiversity through Law No. 5/1990 on conservation of living resources and its ecosystem, laws supporting the ABS system should speed-up the process. Passage of remanded law No. 18/2002 on National Research System, Development, and Implementation of Knowledge and Technology Science gave hardship to foreign researchers

224) Native to Madagascar was introduced as a cancer medicine formula of vincristine. Also known for diabetes, Hodgkin's disease and leukemia use.

225) Native to India and Nepal, W.R. Grace and the company received a European patent in 1994 and revoked later in 2005 since the plant source 'neem' is an Indian traditional medicine.

226) Native to Mexico, blocking of use after receiving patent in1999 caused a 90% drop in the export sale. Then the patent was revoked in 2008.

227) Filing attempt of a patent by the US cooperation RiceTEc (a subsidiary of RiceTec AG of Liechtenstein)using basmatic rice and semidwarf long-grain rice was failed.

228) While documenting the biodiversity of Chiapas, Mexico and ethnobotanical knowledge of the indigenous Maya people, the International Cooperative Biodiversity Group led by ethnobiologist Brent Berlin was accused of being bioprospecting in 1999-2000.

with stringent requirements. ABS ask for fair use of the gene and benefit for all mankind. Research is one of the means of promoting benefits for all mankind.

(3) Trademark and Geographical Indication

TRIPs Art. 22. 1 defines "Geographic indications are, for the purpose of this Agreement, indications which identify a good as originating in the territory of a Member, or a region or locality in that territory, where a given quality, reputation or other characteristic of the good is essentially attributable to its geographic origin".

As early as 1935, the French government regulated geographical indications for wine having 4 levels such as AOC (appellation d'origine contôlée), VQDS (de qualité supérieure), VDPs (vines de pays), VDP (vin de table). During Uruguay round, EC claims to have stronger protections for the geographical indications (GI). However, having a different system for protection for the geographical indication the US opposes the idea. Finally, EC had to settle with 3 articles in the TRIPS. Article 22 for protection of geographical indications, Article 23 for additional protection for geographical indications for wines and spirits, Article 24 for international negotiations and exceptions. In the meantime, EC has provided stronger protection for the geographical indications through EC regulation 2801/92 which governs the protection of GI and designation of origin for agricultural products and foodstuffs. Although EC had to make minor changes on the regulation, the EC-protection of GI and designation of origin for agricultural products and foodstuffs[229]case brought EC much needed confirmation on the EC's GI system by WTO. Using GI as a way of protecting cultural heritage is also desirable having in mind that the relationship between culture and trade can be mutually supportive.

229) WT/DS174/R(March 15, 2005).

Implementation of GI can neither make a change of rights and duties of WTO member states nor infringe legitimate interests of the owner of the trademark and of third parties[230].

230) Park, Jihyun, "Protection of Geographical Indications through TRIPs-Plus", Hanyang Law Review, Vol 22-1, 2011.

14. Toyota Motor Corp v. Nio Teddy Siswanto (LEXUS Trademark Dispute)

Key Principle: Similarity test also applies to trademark dispute in District Court Level

1) Facts

Toyota Motor Corporation (Toyota Jidosha Kabushiki Kaisha) is a Japanese multinational automotive manufacturer[231)]. In 1992, Toyota Motor Corporation registered its trademark "LEXUS & L logo" at the Trademark Directorate, Ministry of Justice of the Republic of Indonesia which later changed to Directorate General of Intellectual Property Indonesia (DJKI) with No. 275.609. Toyota Motor Corporation has its trademark renewal in 2002 under No. 496.408 for class 12 (vehicles) with the purposes to protect cars, auto parts, accessories and etc in Indonesia for distinguishing the result from other parties[232)].

In 2010, Nio Teddy Siswanto an Indonesian businessman submitted a trademark registration to DJKI, the "Lexus" brand for class 2 (paint) with registration No. IDM000248851[233)]. In the same year, Toyota Motor Corporation sued Nio Teddy Siswanto (defendant) along with DJKI (co-defendants) in the Central Jakarta Commercial Court for cancellation of the "Lexus" trademark owned by Nio Teddy in class 2 with registration No. IDM000248851. The lawsuit aims to declare that the plaintiff is the exclusive rights holder of the Lexus trademark No. IDM000248851 in Indonesia and states that the defendant's trademark in words and sound are the same in principle as the plaintiff's trademark.

231) Toyota Motor Corporation produces vehicles under five brands, including Toyota, Hino, Lexus, Ranaz, and Daihatsu.

232) Class 12 is related to automotive parts, to check the Class visit the website http://skm.dgip.go.id.

233) Class 2 is related to paint, to check the Class visit the website http://skm.dgip.go.id.

2) Court Decision

At the district level, decision case No. 80/MEREK/2010/PN.NIAGA. JKT.PST, Court has granted ownership to the plaintiff. The Court held that the plaintiff has an exclusive right of "Lexus & Logo L" Trademark, stating the defendant's trademark No. IDM000248851 in words and voice is the same as the plaintiff's trademark. The court canceled of the defendant's No. IDM000248851 trademark registration with all legal consequences.

3) Comments

(1) Similarity Test and Well-Known Marks/Famous Marks in District Court Level

Plaintiff's trademark is "LEXUS & Logo L" for class 12 and the trademark registered by the defendant is "Lexus" for class 2. In this case, there is a similarity of words and sounds in common between the two brands because they use the same 5 letters i.e. L, E, X, U, S. Based on the explanation of Article 6 paragraph 1 (a) of Law No. 15/2001 on trademarks[234)]:

> "What is meant by similarity in principle is the resemblance caused by the presence of prominent elements between one brand and another, which may give rise to the appearance of similarities in terms of form, method of determination, method of writing or combination of elements or similarities. sound sayings contained in these brand"

Similarity test is the key to this case. Having said that, First, there is a similar use of the alphabet letter especially in sequence consisting

234) Law No.19/1992 on Trademark is the first law on trademark, then amended to Law No.14/1997, after that changed to Law No. 15/2001 on Trademark is the first law concerning trademark, This law was amended to Law No.20/2016 on Trademarks and geographical indications.

of 5 letters L, E, X, U, S[235]. Second, the plaintiff's trademark is a well-known mark/famous mark registered in various countries[236]. Third, the plaintiff's patent application was granted in 1992 and renewed in 2002[237]. Considering these factors, the judge at the district level decided to cancel the trademark registration of the defendant. Article 6 paragraph 1 (b) Law No. 15/2001 on trademarks states;

"The rejection of companies which have similarities in principle or whole with a well-known brand for goods and/or services of the same type is carried out with due regard to the general knowledge of the public about the mark in the business sector concerned. Besides that, it is also noted that the reputation of famous brands has been obtained due to the intense and massive promotion, investment in several countries in the world carried out by the owner. It also is accompanied by proof of registration of the mark in several countries".

---

235) Decision No.80/MEREK/2010/PN.NIAGA.JKT.PST, p.11.
236) *Ibid*, p.14.
237) *Ibid*, p.15.

15. DC Comics, Inc v. PT.Marxing Fam Makmur(Superman Iconic Character as Trademark Dispute)

Key Principle: Inaccurate Power of Attorney combined with several procedure defects can be the basis of the reason for dismissal of the case

1) Facts

Plaintiff, DC Comics, Inc. is one of the largest and oldest American comic book publisher[238]. It is the publishing unit of DC Entertainment[239], a subsidiary of Warner Bros Global Brands and Experiences. The majority of its publications was made in the fictional DC Universe and feature numerous culturally iconic heroic characters, most notably superman, batman and wonder woman, etc. Superman is one of the iconic hero characters of DC Comics with its famous icon and criteria such as his blue uniform, red cape, the "S" shield on his chest, and the title of the man of steel[240]. Superman is of the most immediately recognizable and beloved DC Superheroes of all time to the public[241].

Defendant, PT. Marxing Fam Makmur is a Surabaya-based food and beverage company making chocolate wafer products with the brand name "Superman" accompanied by an image similar to Superman's criteria. Its trademark was registered on April 26, 2016, and trademark newsletter No. 31/VII/A/2017 was announced on July 5, 2017 - October 2017[242].

In 2018, DC Comics (plaintiff) sued PT. Marxing Fam Makmur

238) Wikipedia, *DC Comics*, last modified November 12, 2019, https://en.wikipedia.org/wiki/DC_Comics

239) Kelvin Melrose, *DC Entertainment: What we Know so Far*, last modified November 11, 2019, https://web.archive.org/web/20090913142220/http://robot6.comicbookresources.com/2009/09/dc-entertainment-what-we-know-so-far/

240) DC Comics, *Superman*, last modified November 11, 2019, https://www.dccomics.com/characters/superman

241) DC Comics has not registered its character in Indonesia.

242) The registration of Superman brand by PT.Marxing Fam Makmur No.IDM000374438 and IDM000374439.

(defendant) along with the Directorate General of Intellectual Property of the Republic of Indonesia (co-defendants) in the Central Jakarta Commercial Court. The main point of the lawsuit is (1) Cancellation of the "Superman" trademark and deleting requests for registration of "Superman" trademarks on behalf of the defendant to the co-defendants. (2) Granting of the Superman trademark on behalf of the plaintiff and issuance of a certificate by the co-defendant.

2) Court Decision

At the district level, the court decision case No. 17/Pdt.Sus-HKI/ Merek/2018/PN.Niaga.Jkt.Pst. granted partially for Defendant's and co-Defendant's exception[243]. The reason for dismissal (Exception)[244] from the Defendant (PT. PT.Marxing Fam Makmur) is[245] :

(1) The Power of Attorney did not meet the formal requirements;
(2) An expired lawsuit of cancellation trademark;
(3) Lawsuit Error in persona in the form of fewer parties (*exceptio plurium litis consortium*);
(4) The lawsuit is too early (premature);and
(5) The lawsuit is vague and unclear (exceptio obscuur libel).

Then, the Co-defendant's Exception (DJKI KEMENKUMHAM RI) is:

1) Expired; and
2) A lawsuit cannot be the object of a dispute.

243) In this case, when the case is dismissed a lawsuit is closed without further looking into the matters in controversy, controversy on the merits.
244) In the Indonesian legal term, the reason for dismissal in a court proceeding is called 'exception' (in Bahasa: Eksepsi).
245) The lawsuit can be checked in case No. 17/Pdt.Sus-Merek/2018/PN.Niaga.Jkt.Pst and Case No. 1105k/Pdt.Sus-HKI/2018, p.3.

At Court of Cassation, the judge rejected a request of inter-retaliation of relevant laws and ordered DC Comics to pay the court fee in cassation rate Rp. 5.000.000,- (five million rupiah).

3) Comments

(1) Claim of Missing Formal Requirement

Plaintiff argued that the defendant's power of attorney did not meet the formal requirement. A power of attorney is used for the authority of the attorney to represent the grantor. In this case, the lawsuit includes cancellation of the Superman trademark owned by the defendant and DC comics also requested the issuance of the Superman trademark certificate on behalf of the plaintiff. But the plaintiff's attorney attached the power of attorney that is only for the cancellation of the Superman trademark so that the receiver of the power of attorney (plaintiff lawyer) has committed acts that exceed the authority given by the grantor (DC Comics on behalf of Brenda C. Karickhoof as senior Vice-President). In the end, the judge handed down the judgment saying the power of attorney did not fulfill the formal requirements.

In the court proceedings, after the plaintiff read its lawsuit in front of the judges then the defendant asked for the application of the exception on the judges[246)]. The exception submitted by the defendant and co-defendant said the Plaintiff's claim is vague and unclear because the contents of the plaintiff is a combination of cancellation and the issuance of the certificate. Then the judges granted a partial exception to the defendant[247)].

(2) Well-Known Trademark

DC Comics claims that the DC Comics have exclusive rights to the Superman brands, the S logo and Superman paintings/drawings DC Comics in the territory of Indonesia. In this case, DC Comics is a well-known comic publisher in America as well as other countries. The characters

246) In Indonesia, civil proceedings, exception or answer (suspicion) in the civil case of the defendant is not addressed to the subject matter, but if it turns out to be true then it can result in the failure of the lawsuit.

247) Supreme Court Decision No. 1105K/Pdt.Sus-HKI/2018, p.5.

and products made by DC Comics are well known throughout the world, especially the Superman character.

First, Superman is an iconic hero well known to all now. Second, superman images have been registered together with Action Comics 1 in 1938[248]. Third, a writer Jerry Siegel and artist, Joe Shuster who made the Supermen character in 1930 was already famous in the U.S. That Superman can be said as a well-known mark or famous mark[249]. The famous mark argument could have been a strong legal argument for the plaintiff in the court because Superman mark is a famous character in the world as an iconic hero owned by DC Comics. DC Comics could have won the case if the defendant used the well-known trademark protection defense guaranteed under the Law No.20/2016 on Trademarks and geographical indications. But the plaintiff did not have a chance to prove it because the court granted the exception to the defendant.

248) Catalog of Copyright Entries 1938 Periodicals Jan-Dec New Series Vol 33, p.2, last modified November 11, 2019 https://archive.org/stream/catalogofcopyrig332lib#page/n141/mode/2up.

249) Well-known marks are usually protected, irrespective of whether they are registered or not, in respect of goods and services which are identical with, or similar to, those for which they have gained their reputation.

16. HUGO BOSS v. Teddy Tan & Alexander (HUGO BOSS Trademark Dispute)

Key Principle: Implementation of Simmilarity test into Trademark dispute in Cassation Level

1) Facts

HUGO BOSS is a German luxury fashion house headquartered in Metzingen. It was founded in 1924. In 1925, the HUGO BOSS developed their product under HUGO BOSS BRAND[250]. HUGO BOSS has registered in various countries such as Germany, Taiwan, Hong Kong, Singapore and Australia, etc. In Indonesia itself, HUGO BOSS also registered at the DJKI for the first time in classes 3, 18, 24, and 25 on January 24, 1999[251].

Teddy Tan, an Indonesian businessman who engages in the fashion clothing which has a HUGO SPORT brand has registered its trademark at DJKI for class 25. the HUGO SPORT brand has been registered to No. IDM000345958, Hugo to No. IDM000156404, and HUGO SPORT + painting to No. IDM000248526 since 2001.

Alexander, an Indonesian businessman who engages in the fashion clothing which has a ZEGOBOSS brand has registered at the DJKI for class 25 with register No.IDM000189607, No.000394982, ZEGOBOSS PLATINUM + LOGO No.IDM000384747 and No. IDM000376735 for class 3 since 2009.

In 2016, HUGO BOSS, represented by HUGO BOSS Trade Mark Management GmbH and Co.KG, sued Alexander and Teddy Tan along with DJKI (co-defendants) at the Central Jakarta District Court for the purpose

250) In 1988 added fragrance, 1997 added men's and womenswear, 2000 added full women's collection, 2006/2007 as well as children's clothing, and in 2016 it owned more than 1,100 retail stores worldwide and every year always have a new brand of ide fashion design.

251) Class 3 is related to perfume, Class 18 is related to travel things, Class 24 is related to fabric products, Class 25 is related to clothing and Class 35 is related to wholesale, to check the Class visit the website http://skm.dgip.go.id.

of cancelling several marks registered under Alexander and Teddy Tan in separate case numbers[252)]. The main cause of action in the HUGO BOSS lawsuit are:

(1) Declare the Plaintiff (HUGO BOSS) is the first owner and registrant entitled to use the HUGO BOSS mark and its variations in Indonesia;

(2) Declare that the HUGO BOSS brand and its variations belong to the claimant as a well-known brand/famous brand;

(3) The ZEGOBOSS brand with its variations belong to Alexander and the HUGO SPORT brand with the variations belong to Teddy Tan has a similarity with the Plaintiff's trademark;

(4) Registration of the ZEGOBOSS trademark with its variations belong to Alexander and the HUGO SPORTS mark with the variations owned by Teddy Tan are registered based on bad faith;

(5) Cancel the ZEGOBOSS brand with its variations belonging to Alexander and the HUGO SPORT brand with the variations that belong to Teddy Tan.

2) Court Decision

At district court level, case No. 27/Pdt.Sus-HKI/2016/PN.Niaga.Jkt.Pst, the court rejected the plaintiff's lawsuit entirely and imposed the cost of the case to the plaintiff.

At district court level, case No. 30/Pdt.Sus-HKI/2016/PN.Niaga.Jkt.Pst, the court rejected the plaintiff's lawsuit entirely and imposed the cost of the case to the plaintiff.

At cassation court level, case No. 92 K/Pdt.Sus-HKI/2017, the court

252) HUGO BOSS v. Alexander in case No. 27/Pdt.Sus-HKI/2016/PN.JKT.PST and HUGO BOSS v. Teddy Tan in case No.30/Pdt.Sus-HKI/2016/PN.JKT.PST.

granted the cassation petition. The cassation court decision resulted in canceling the decision of the first level district court case No. 30/Pdt.Sus/HKI/2016/PN.Niaga.Jkt.Pst and granting the Plaintiff's lawsuit.

At cassation court level, decision case No. 938 K/Pdt.Sus-HKI/2017, the court granted the cassation petition. The cassation court decision resulted in canceling the decision of the first level district court case No. 26/Pdt.Sus-HKI/2016/PN.Niaga.Jkt.Pst and granting the Plaintiff's lawsuit.

At Judicial Review level, case No. 217 PK/Pdt.Sus-HKI/2018, the court rejected the Judicial Review request from the Applicant (Teddy Tan) and punished the applicant to pay the court examination fee for Judicial Review.

3) Comments

(1) Similarity test and Well Know Marks/Famous Marks at Cassation Level

At the cassation court level, the Supreme Court Judge handed down verdict saying that the district court has incorrectly applied and rejected its interpretation of the provisions of law No. 20/2016 on Trademarks and Geographical Indications by saying that the trademarks cannot be registered when the trademark resembles the name or abbreviation of the name of a famous person, photo, or the name of a legal entity owned by another person, with exception of the written consent of the entitled person[253].

The HUGO BOSS trademark (plaintiff) has a similar alphabet letter with ZEGO BOSS trademark (defendant, alexander) consisting of B, O, S, S. as well as HUGO SPORT (defendant, teddy tan) consisting of H, U, G,O. Similar alphabets are prominent elements of HUGO BOSS which is also used at ZEGO BOSS and HUGO SPORT.

253) Article 21 verse 2(a) of Law No. 20 of 2016 about Trademarks and geographical indications.

At the district court level, in both cases of alexander (ZEGO BOSS) and teddy tan (HUGO SPORT), the district judge did not consider or at least not provided sufficient legal considerations relating to the similarity between the HUGO BOSS and ZEGO BOSS and HUGO SPORT. District court judge errored in applying the similarity test to trademark. The court concludes:

(1) The HUGO BOSS brands and their variations are well-known trademarks of the defendant;

(2) The HUGO BOSS brand and its variations since 1924 have been produced by the trademark rights holders and started investing in Indonesia since 1990;

(3) The HUGO BOSS brand has been registered in several countries and is a well-known trademark. Therefore, using the words "HUGO" and "BOSS" in a trademark that does not belong to the defendant or variations of the plaintiff's HUGO BOSS is an act of free-riding that can mislead the customer and cause harm to the plaintiff;

(4) The words "HUGO" and "BOSS" of the plaintiff do not have a general understanding so that other brands owned by the defendant that have the same words "HUGO" and "BOSS" give a strong impression that the two products are from the same company. The words "HUGO" and "BOSS" are the dominant/prominent elements in the brand;

(5) The defendant used the words "HUGO" and "BOSS" on his trademark, giving the appearance of similarity in principle to the plaintiff's famous brand;

(6) That the equation is about the form and equation of the sound of words in the word which is the dominant element of the words "HUGO" and "BOSS" in the brand;

(7) The word "HUGO BOSS" is part of the plaintiff's legal entity HUGO BOSS Trade Mark Management GmbH & Co.KG and is a

trademark of its product.

The Supreme Court judge in the cassation level considered the prominent words in the trademark. The alphabet "HUGO" and "BOSS" has a prominent similarity in both trademarks "ZEGO BOSS" and "HUGO SPORT". The judge also considered whether that the brand "HUGO BOSS" is a well-known mark / famous mark that has been registered in several countries and many people know the mark or not.

17. Inter IKEA System B.V. v. PT. Ratania Khatulistiwa (IKEA Trademark Dispute)

Key Principle: The statutory requirement of three-year consecutive non-use of trademark results in cancellation of IP rights

1) Facts

IKEA is a company owned by Inter IKEA Systems B.V., registered in Sweden founded in 1943[254]. In 2014, Inter IKEA Systems submitted an application for trademark registration to the DJKI including the "IKEA" brand for class 21 in 2006 with the registration No. IDM000092006,[255] and the "IKEA" brand for class 20 in 2010 with registration No. IDM000277901[256].

PT. Ratania Khatulistiwa is an official Indonesian legal entity company[257]. In 2013, PT.Ratania Khatulistiwa submitted two applications for trademark registration to DJKI, the "ikea" brand for class 21 with application No. D002013061336 and the "ikea" brand for class 20 with the application No. D002013061337[258].

In the same year PT.Ratania Khatulistiwa sued Inter IKEA system B.V. (defendant) along with DJKI (co-defendants) in the Central Jakarta Commercial Court to remove the "IKEA" trademark owned by Inter IKEA System B.V. in class 20 and 21 with registration numbers IDM00092006

254) The main business is selling assemble furniture, kitchen appliances and home accessories, among other useful goods and occasionally home services and founded in Sweden in 1943, for Further Information on IKEA, visit the official website on https://about.ikea.com.

255) Class 21 is related to household utensils, to check the Class visit the website http://skm.dgip.go.id.

256) Class 20 is related to household furniture, to check the Class visit the website http://skm.dgip.go.id.

257) The main business is in the manufacture of wood and rattan furniture industry located in Surabaya-East Java, which was established in 1989, for further information of PT.Ratania Khatulistiwa, visit the official website on http://www.ratania.com.

258) The trademark "ikea" registered by PT.Ratania is an abbreviation of the words 'Intan', 'Khatulistiwa', 'Esa', and 'Abadi' in Indonesian.

and IDM000277901, as well as filing an application for the acceptance of the "ikea" brand trademark of PT. Ratania Khatulistiwa in classes 20 and 21 with application No. D002013061337 and D002013061336.

2) Court Decision

At district court level, case No. 99/Pdt.Sus-HKI/2013/PN.JKT.PST, The court granted the plaintiff's claim.

> "... 5. Declare the "IKEA" trademark registered under the name Inter IKEA System BV (defendant) with registration number IDM000277901 registration date 27 October 2010 for goods/ services class 20 and IDM000092006 registration number 9 October 2006 registration date for goods/services class 21, not used during class 21 3 years in a row in the trade in goods and/or services from the date of registration.
>
> ... 7. Declare the deletion of the "IKEA" brand registered under the name Inter IKEA System BV (defendant) with registration number IDM000277901 registration date 27 October 2010 for goods/ services class 20 and IDM000092006 registration number 9 October 2006 registration date for goods/services class 21 from the public register trademark DJKI with all the legal consequences".

The Court approved the removal of the trademark "IKEA" registered by Inter IKEA System B.V, in class 20 and 21because of the non-use of the trademark within the statutory period of 3 consecutive years after registration[259]. Therefore "IKEA" Trademark in class 20 and 21 were canceled and "ikea" got the ownership of the trademark in class 20 and 21, however. "IKEA" still owned and hold the exclusive right of the trademark in other classes.

259) Art 61 verses 2(a) of Law No. 15/2001 on Trademark.

The proof of the non-use of the "IKEA" brand owned by the defendant (Inter Ikea System B.V.) in classes 20 and 21 for 3 years in a row is evidenced by the results of a survey conducted by Berlian Group Indonesia[260], and the plaintiff used the survey result it as the evidence at the court trial in district court level.

In cassation level, case No. 264 K/Pdt.Sus-HKI/2015, The court rejected the cassation request from the cassation applicant (Inter Ikea System B.V.) and sentenced the cassation applicant to pay the court fee in the cassation rate of Rp.5,000,000. (five million rupiahs). The court rejected the cassation request because the supreme court didn't find any mistakes in the central Jakarta district court decision as the central commercial court has applied Law No. 15/2001 on Trademark as the legal basis for the court decision.

3) Comments

(1) Non-Use Cancellation

There is revised trademark Law No. 20/2016. However, this IKEA case was brought to court in 2013. therefore, the court used trademark law No. 15/2001. Indonesia has a "First to File" rule for obtaining trademark rights instead of "first to invent"[261], where exclusive rights will be given to the first registrar. Also, the principle of territoriality, that is, the exclusive rights of a mark only apply in the territory of the country where the mark is registered. So, multinational companies need to register their brands in the countries where they conduct their business activities.

Through non-use cancellation, the DJKI requires the registered trademark owner to use it in the goods/services within the statutory period of 3 consecutive years after registration. PT.Ratania Khatulistiwa used the

260) Berlian Group Indonesia is a private intelligence service business group, especially for market surveys.

261) First to file is Principle are legal concepts that define who has the right to the grant of IPR.

condition of non-use to sue Inter IKEA System B.V., in a removal suit in which the plaintiff requested that an already registered trademark be deleted from the public register of trademarks on the grounds that one of them has not been used for 3 consecutive years after legislation[262]. The legal issue of the non-use is based on Article 61 of Law No. 15/2001 on Trademark.

> "Removal of trademark registration on the initiative of the Directorate General can be done if:
> a. The brand is not used for 3 (three) consecutive years in the trade in goods and/or services from the date of registration or last use, except if there are reasons that can be accepted by the Directorate General; or
> b. Brands are used for types of goods and/or services that are not in accordance with the types of goods or services requested for registration, including the use of Marks that are incompatible with the Marks registered."

The decision does not mean that the transfer of rights and ownership of the removed IKEA to PT. Ratania Khatulistiwa, because the claim for brand removal is not for competition for ownership of the trademark but for removing the trademark from certain conditions. In this case, the Inter IKEA System brand "IKEA" has been abolished and the "ikea" brand owned by PT. Ratania Khatulistiwa was successfully registered at DJKI. Even though the names of the two brands are the same, it does not mean that the newest brand "ikea" registered takes fame and popularity from the brand name that was previously "IKEA".

262) Prayudi Setiadharma, *Sedikit Kisah Tentang Hapusnya Merek IKEA*, last modified November 11, 2019, http://www.hki.co.id/opini/ikea.

18. John Hardy Jewelry & PT. Karya Tangan Indah v. Ketut Deni Aryasa(Traditional Bali "Folklore" Motifs Dispute)

Key Principle: Craft design representing folklore that is in public domain can be used even by foreigner

1) Facts

Ketut Deni Aryasa is a traditional Bali silver craftsman and entrepreneur. Ketut Deni Aryasa has exported traditional Bali silver handicraft products. In 2008, Ketut Deni Aryasa was accused of infringing copyright by plagiarizing the work of silver jewelry of US-Canada entrepreneurs (John Hardy Jewelry and PT. Karya Tangan Indah). Ketut Deni Aryasa used *fleur & crocodile* that are traditional Balinese tribal motifs that can be found in almost all art ornaments in Bali culture. The Balinese people have been using the motif freely as a form of Balinese cultural expression.

John Hardy, a Canadian designer and artist founded John Hardy Jewelry[263). John Hardy Jewelry was inspired by Bali jewelry and he learned the techniques from the local Bali artisan then he established his business in Bali in 1975. The main business focused on handcrafted jewelry. PT. Karya Tangan Indah is an Indonesian, company which is the manufacturer of John Hardy products. In 2006, PT. Karya Tangan Indah registered the copyright of fleur motif in DJKI with registration No. 030376 including the description that the creator of *fleur* motif is Guy Rainer Gabrial Bedarida, a France citizenship who living in Bali-Indonesia[264). Then in 2008 John Hardy Jewelry and PT. Karya Tangan Indah sued Ketut Deni Aryasa for plagiarism and copyright infringement.

---

263) Check for detail of John Hardy's business on the website https://www.johnhardy.com.

264) International Law in News,"Berebut Hasil Kreasi Pengrajin Perak Bali", *Jurnal Hukum International*, Vol.6 No.1, October 2008, p.158.

2) Court Decision

At the district court level, Ketut Deni Aryasa was not proven guilty of copyright infringement, because the judges did not find any similar aspect in the disputed product especially the *Fluer & Crocodile* motifs during court proceedings.

The judge's decision was influenced by the witness's expertise in court. Tjokorda Udiana Nindia Pemayun S.SN., SH., M.Hum, a Lecturer of Institut Seni Indonesia Denpasar (Art Indonesia Institution) stated that:

"The work of different basic ideas is not possible to make the same results, all influenced by the substantial elements of the product, such as the type of material, the pouring process, motives and textures."

3) Comments

(1) Protection of Traditional Expression Culture (Folklore)

Copyright is a form of protection intend to protect the intangible creation or original expression of an idea in the form of intellectual work in Indonesia[265]. The motifs attached to the traditional Balinese silver handicraft is covered by copyright. The motifs used by the Balinese craftsmen are inherent in the ethnic Balinese community, so they become a cultural expression inherent to generations of Balinese people without knowing who the creators of these traditional motifs are. Now motifs become the public domain of the Balinese people and are free to use it.

The Expression of Traditional Culture especially the traditional motifs of silver Bali is protected by the Copyright Law and the State which holds the Copyright on works for prehistoric relics, history and other national cultural objects, Folklore and the products of the people's

265) Kadek Julia Mahadewi, "Budaya Hukum dalam Keberlakuan Undang-Undang Nomor 28 Tahun 2014 tentang Hak Cipta Pada Pengrajin Perak Di Bali", *Udayana Master Law Journal*, Vol.4, No.2, July 2015, p.206.

cultural traditions. It is now in the public domain of Balinese people[266]. To announce or reproduce the creation of folklore if non-Indonesian citizens want, he/she must first obtain permission from the agency concerned in the matter[267]. However, there are other cases. For example, the fluid motive that is an expression of traditional Balinese culture is owned by foreign citizens.

In 2014, Law No. 28/2014 on Copyright strengthened the protection of traditional expression culture (folklore). New Copyright Law protects folklore owned by the state without any expiration date. For the use of traditional cultural expressions, one must pay attention to the values that live in the developing society[268]. The goal of protection is the compilation of traditional cultural expressions as long as the compilation is an original work[269].

266) Art 10 (2) of Law No. 19/2002 on Copyright Law, Because the cases above held in 2008, so used the old version of Indonesia Copyright Law.

267) Art 10 (3) of Law no.19/2002 on Copyright Law (Old version of Indonesia Copyright Law).

268) Art. 39 of Law no.28/2014 on Copyright law. What is meant by traditional cultural expression includes one or a combination of forms of textual verbal expression, music, movement, theater, 2D and/or 3D fine art, traditional ceremonies

269) Art. 40 verse 1(p) of Law No.28/2014 on Copyright.

19. Indonesia Monkey Selfie Picture Dispute

Key Principle: Animal does not own Copyright

1) Facts

In 2011, a British photographer David J. Slater traveled to a National Park in North Sulawesi, Indonesia. David J. Slater took pictures of the local wild in the National Park of North Sulawesi. He claims that he was specifically looking for a very close shot of a monkey's face using a wide-angle lens of one monkey named Naruto. Her name like the sound that sounded the name of some character from the Japan Manga series. But it was actually was named by local guardian officer of National Park's[270)], was obviously shy and didn't allow him to get too close. David slater placed his camera on a tripod as the monkey was curious about the equipment and clicked the camera trigger and took a few pictures. One of these images was astounding since it captured an expression of pure joy and self-awareness on the monkey himself[271)]. Naruto snapped several photos of himself with a camera that belongs to the photographer David J. Salter, who was on assignment in Indonesia.

The picture of the monkey selfie picture was first published by the daily mail as a feature story and then went viral. Then the picture was used in the Wikipedia website, with a description self-portrait of a female Macaque Nigra. In 2011, several publications including daily mail, the Telegraph

270) The Monkey is Female Crested Black Macaque Monkey.

271) Andres Guadamuz, *WIPO MAGAZINE*, last modified November 17, 2019 , https://www.wipo.int/wipo_magazine/en/2018/01/article_0007.html.

and the Guardian published the story with the pictures that quoted slater as describing the photographs as self-portraits taken by the monkeys "Monkey steals camera to snap himself" (The Telegraph), "A camera on a tripod triggered by the monkey" (The Guardian), and a camera started by a monkey "Fascinated by her reflection in the lens and the picture"[272]. Later on, David J. Salter had published a book title "Wildlife Personalities" through San Francisco based publishing company Blurb.

2) Court Decision

In 2015, People for the Ethical Treatment of Animals (PETA) filed a lawsuit against David Salter and Blurb as the publisher in the Northern District of California U.S. claiming that the monkey should be the copyright holder and the PETA should be appointed to administer proceeds from the photos for the benefit of the monkey (naruto) as well as other crested macaques in a nature reserve of the National park in North Sulawesi.

US Court of Appeals for the Ninth Circuit[273], dismissed copyright ownership claims brought by PETA over selfies using wildlife photographer's unattended camera. The court held that the animal cannot own a copyright under U.S. law[274].

During the Appeal process, the PETA and David Slater reached a settlement that David J. Slater would donate 25% of any future revenue derived from using or selling the monkey selfie to wildlife organization that protects the crested Macaques habitat in Indonesia[275].

272) Wikipedia, *Monkey Selfie Copyright*, last modified November 17, 2019, https://en.wikipedia.org/wiki/Monkey_selfie_copyright_dispute.

273) Case Number 16-15469. D.D.No. 3:15-cv-04324-WHO.

274) The original court decision case can be found at Law Justia Website: https://law.justia.com/cases/federal/appellate-courts/ca9/16-15469/16-15469-2018-04-23.html.

275) Sussanah Cullinane, *Monkey Does Not Own Selfie Copyright, Appeals Court Rules*, last modified 17 November 2019, https://edition.cnn.com/2018/04/24/us/monkey-selfie-peta-appeal/index.html.

3) Comments

(1) Jurisdiction

Even after the settlement between the two parties, the court of appeals declined to dismiss the appeal. In April 2018, the appeal court confirm that animals do not have a legal ground of copyrights. Indonesian copyright law does not recognize animal owning the copyright. Although a monkey selfie was taken in Indonesia territory, the monkey cannot own the copyright under Indonesia law. Picture taken through photographic works can be an object of Indonesian copyright law if Indonesian have taken the picture.

> Article 1 verses 2 of Indonesia Copyright Law No.28 of 2014 says "Creator is a person or group who individually or jointly produce a unique and personal creation."
>
> Article 40 verses (k) of Indonesia Copyright Law No.28 of 2014 says, "Photography work's categorize as works protected by this copyright law."

The Case took place in a California court because David Slater has published a book called *"Wildlife Personalities"* using the self-publishing service Blurb inc. The Plaintiffs (PETA) claimed that this is enough to grant them standing in the United States for the Jurisdiction and used United State copyright law[276)]. The court granted subject matter jurisdiction.

Although the picture was shared on the internet and already used by others for certain purposes such as publication, the jurisdiction of the case can be complex considering the element of cyberspace.

The domicile of David J. Slater is the United Kingdom and as a British citizen, any future litigation can take in the United Kingdom. In

276) Andres Guadamuz, *Op.Cit.*.

addition, the Berne Convention for the Protection of Literary and Artistic Works (1886) stipulates the origin of work[277]. Article 5 of verses Berne Convention says;

> "Authors shall enjoy, in respect protected under this Convention, in countries of the union other than the country of origin, the rights which their respective laws do now or may hereafter grant to their nationals, as well as the rights specially granted by this convention".

Article 5 of verses (2) Berne Convention says;

> "The enjoyment and the exercise of these rights shall not be subject to any formality, such enjoyment and such exercise shall be independent of the existence of protection in the country of origin of the work consequently, apart from the provisions of this convention, the extent of protection, as well as the means of redress afforded to the author to protect his rights, shall be governed exclusively by the laws of the country where protection is claimed."

In this case, the picture was taken in Indonesia by David Slater camera, and first published in the UK through Caters News Agency which granted permission for its publication in the British media then published a personal book in the U.S. So, the copyright is owned by David J. Selter as the photographer. There is no copyright law that gives ownership of copyright to animals in the world including Indonesia. Some scholars in the United States and the United Kingdom insisted on the recognition of animal/non-human as the copyright holder[278].

277) The Berne Convention, adopted in 1886, deals with the protection of works and the rights of their authors. It provides creators such as authors, musicians, poets, painters, etc. with the means to control how their works are used, by whom, and on what terms. It is based on three basic principles and contains a series of provisions determining the minimum protection to be granted, as well as special provisions available to developing countries that want to make use of them.

278) Other opinions from scholars claim that no human author has rights to a photograph taken by a monkey so the monkey selfie picture belongs to the public domain.

Part VI
Human Rights Cases

20. Rawagede 1948

21. Massacare 1965

22. Aceh Conflict Resolution

23. Indonesia Reformation 1998

24. Sampit Conflict 2001

25. Bali Bombing 2002

26. Death Sentenced for International Drug Traffikers

27. Aceh LGBT Cases

28. Chandra and others v. Netherlands

29. Mc.Donald House Bombing

VI Human Rights Cases

20. Rawagede Case 1948(Wisah Binti Silan et.al v. The State of Netherlands)

Key Principle: Execution without proper due process and killing civilian without distinguishing them from combatant is a breach of International humanitarian law(IHL) as well as customary IHL

1) Facts

Indonesia was colonized by the Netherland empire for nearly 350 years. After declaration of independence on August 17, 1945, Netherland tried to re-occupy Indonesia with the allies making a pretense to wipe the Japanese Imperial Defense Force. Indonesia called this historic event 'Netherland Aggression I' on July 21, 1947 – Aug 4, 1947. It is internationally called 'Operation Product' and 'Netherland II Aggression (Operation Crow)' or 'Operation Kraai' in the Netherland language, on Dec 19, 1948 – Dec 20, 1948.

Netherland Aggression against Indonesia created scars for many Indonesian. One of the accidents was the Rawagede massacre during Netherland Aggression I or Operation Product. This case is well documented in United Nations Security Council Document Number S/649/Corr.1 dated 12 February 1948 titled Committee of Good Offices on the Indonesian question which stated the accident in Rawagede caused 300 civilians deaths and 200 injuries.[279)] Nearly after 60 years of the case, the family of the Rawagede case victim sued the government of the Netherland in the district court of the Hague, Netherland in 2008. The decision came down in 2011[280)].

279) United Nations Security Council Document Number S/649/Corr.1 12 February 1948, last modified April 27, 2020, https://digitallibrary.un.org/record/469227?ln=en.

280) Irvan Setiawan, *Peristiwa Tragedi Berdarah Rawagede*, Kementrian Pendidikan dan Kebu-

2) Court Decision

The Foundation of the committee of Dutch Honorary Debt translated this incident into the English language[281)] and the Hague District Court found that the state of Netherland acted unlawfully toward plaintiff Wisah Binti Silan, Wanti Binti Dodo, Lasmi Binti Kasilan, Cawi Binti Baisan Taswi, Tijeng Binti Tasim, Layem Binti Murkin by executing their spouses and towards Saih Bin Sakam by gunning him down[282)]. The Court then ordered the State of Netherland to pay the legal cost[283)]. The Court ordered Taijsi Binti Tikin and the Foundation of Committee of Dutch Honorary Debt to pay the legal cost to the state for the trial and dismissed other applications[284)].

3) Comments

(1) Customary Rules of Humanitarian Law[285)]

The sources of IHL are treaties, customs and the general principles of law. Soft law such as international cases, domestic cases, international organization documents, doctrine, in practices plays a role in the interpretation. A collection of customary rules of humanitarian law are practical guidelines given by the ICRC and reflection of practice in the field

---

dayaan, November 10, 2018, last modified april 27, 2020, https://kebudayaan.kemdikbud.go.id/bpnbjabar/peristiwa-tragedi-berdarah-rawagede/.

281) The original decision of this case is in the Dutch language, but the Foundation of Committee of Dutch Honorary Debt (in Bahasa: Komite Hutang Kehormatan Belanda) with the help of Guy Schuitemaker, a sworn translator of Dutch-English, English Dutch translated it.

282) Foundation of Committee of Dutch Honorary Debt, Translated version of District of Hague Court Decision case number/docket number: 354119 / HA ZA 09-4171 14 September 2011, last modified April 27, 2020, http://www.kukb.nl/new/files/Vonnis14092011_EN.pdf .

283) *Ibid.*

284) *Ibid.*

285) Jean-Marie Henckaerts and Louise Doswald-Beck, *Customary International Humanitarian Law*(Vol. I: Rules; Vol II: Practice-part), ICRC, Cambridge University Press (2005). After 10years of the research collection, ICRC distributed the book on the customary International humanitarian law. Total 161 rules are explained with details of field practice.

in 2005. Although parties to the treaties such as the Geneva Convention 1949 or Hauge Convention have an obligation to fulfill the duty enlisted in the convention, customary rules are part of customary international law that comes from "a general practice accepted as law" and exist independent of treaty law. Rules of the customary IHL reflects the principles of IHL.

There are 6 principles that IHL relies on. i) the principle of distinction between civilians and combatants ii) prohibition of attacks against those *horse de combat* iii) prohibition on the infliction of unnecessary suffering iv) proportionality v) notion of necessity vi) humanity.

(1) Rule 1 of the Customary International Humanitarian Law. Parties to a conflict shall at all times distinguish between the civilian population and combatants to spare civilian population and property. Neither the civilian population as such nor civilian persons shall be the object of attack. Attacks shall be directed solely against military objectives[286].

(2) Rule 47 of Customary International Humanitarian Law. It is forbidden to kill or injure an enemy who surrenders or who is *hors de combat*[287].

(3) Rule 70 of Customary International Humanitarian Law. Parties to a conflict and members of their armed forces do not have an unlimited choice of methods and means of warfare. It is prohibited to employ weapons or methods of warfare of a nature to cause unnecessary losses or excessive suffering[288].

Besides, there are also the basic rules of humanitarian law that must

286) See Article 48 of the 1977 Additional Protocol I of Geneva Convention 1949.
287) See Article 3(1) of Geneva Conventions 1949.
288) See United Nations Convention on Certain Conventional Weapons 1980 consisted of 4 Protocol, Protocol I: Non-Detectable Fragments, Protocol II: Mines, Booby Traps and Other Devices, Protocol III: Incendiary Weapons, Protocol IV: Blinding Laser Weapons.

be followed by every combatant through the International customary Law and much of the rules are being formalized in Geneva Convention 1949 and another international law instrument such as Hague Convention. International Committee of Red Cross (ICRC) resume some of the basic rules of Humanitarian law[289]:

(4) Rule 87 of Customary International Humanitarian Law. "Persons *hors de combat* and those who do not take a direct part in hostilities are entitled to respect for their lives and their moral and physical integrity. They shall in all circumstances be protected and treated humanely without any adverse distinction"[290]. During the research on the Customary International Humanitarian law, it became clear that there is no clear distinction between the people "who participate in a direct part in hostilities". There is no definition of "who participate at a direct part in hostilities" either in international conflict or non-international conflict situation. Besides, practice is mixed considering them a civilian or combat in a non-international conflict situation. This is partly because there is no clear definition of the civilian persons in the Additional protocol II[291].

(5) Rule 110 of Customary International Humanitarian Law. The wounded, sick and shipwrecked must receive, to the fullest extent practicable and with the least possible delay, the medical care and attention required by their condition. No distinction may be made among them founded on any grounds other than medical ones[292].

(6) Rule 106 of Customary International Humanitarian Law. Captured

289) International Committee of the Red Cross, Basic rules of the Geneva Conventions and their Additional Protocols, ICRC publication 1988 ref. 0365, p.1., last modified April 27, 2020, https://www.icrc.org/en/doc/assets/files/other/icrc_002_0365.pdf.

290) See Article 3 of the Geneva Conventions 1949.

291) In 2009, ICRC published interpretive guidance on the notion of 'direct participation in hostilities' under International Humanitarian Law written by Nils Melzer, the legal adviser of ICRC in 2009.

292) See Article 6 of Geneva Convention 1864.

combatants and civilians under the authority of an adverse party are entitled to respect for their lives, dignity, personal rights and convictions. They shall be protected against all acts of violence and reprisals. They shall have the right to correspond with their families and to receive relief[293).]

(7) Rule 100 of Customary International Humanitarian Law. Everyone shall be entitled to benefit from fundamental judicial guarantees. No one shall be held responsible for an act he has not committed. No one shall be subjected to physical or mental torture, corporal punishment or cruel or degrading treatment[294)]. Widely known as rule 100 of Customary Humanitarian Law.

(2) Distinction from civilian to combatant

There is an obligation to distinguish between combatant and civilian. According to Rule 1 of Customary International Humanitarian Law and IHL, the parties to the conflict must at all times distinguish between civilians and combatants[295)]. Attacks may only be directed against combatants. Attacks must not be directed against civilians. According to IHL rule 3, Combatants are All members of the armed forces of a party to the conflict, except medical and religious personnel[296)]. Furthermore, according to Rule 4, the armed forces of a party to the conflict consist of all organized armed forces, groups and units that are under a command responsible to that party for the conduct of its subordinates[297)].

Different from a combatant, civilians are persons who are not members

293) See Article 12 of Geneva Convention 1949.
294) See Article 49 Paragraph 4 of Geneva Convention 1949.
295) Formalized in Article 48 Additional Protocol I 1977 of Geneva Convention 1949.
296) Formalized in Article 43(2) of the 1977 Additional Protocol I.
297) Formalized in Article 4(A) of The Geneva Convention III 1949, Add with Additional Protocol I 1977 in Article 43(1) and Additional Protocol II 1977 Article 1(1).

of the armed forces[298]. The civilian population comprises all persons who are civilians, although according to Rule 6 of IHL civilians are protected against attack, unless and for such time as they take a direct part in hostilities[299].

In IHL Rule 7 to 10, the parties to the conflict must at all times distinguish between civilian objects and military objectives. Attacks may only be directed against military objectives. Attacks must not be directed against civilian objects (rule 7)[300]. In so far as objects are concerned, military objectives are limited to those objects which by their nature, location, purpose or use make an effective contribution to military action and whose partial or total destruction, capture or neutralization, in the circumstances ruling at the time, offers a definite military advantage (rule 8)[301]. Civilian objects are all objects that are not military objectives (rule 9)[302], Civilian objects are protected against attack, unless and for such time as they are military objectives (rule 10)[303]. Under Rule 156 of IHL, every serious violation of international humanitarian law constitutes war crimes[304].

Killing protected civilian such as spouses, in this case, is a breach of the Article 13(3) of Additional Protocol II. Person who does not take a direct part in hostilities are the object that the IHL protects and distinguish. Netherland military did breach an obligation to distinguish, at all times, between civilian person and combatants. It is a breach of the Geneva Convention as well as a breach of the Customary International Humanitarian Law.

---

298) Formalized in Article 50 of Additional Protocol I 1977.
299) Formalized in Article 3 of Geneva Convention 1949.
300) Formalized in Article 77 of 1977 Additional Protocol I.
301) Formalized in Article 52(2) of the 1977 Additional Protocol I.
302) Formalized in Article 52(1) of the 1977 Additional Protocol I.
303) Did not Formalized yet, but in some Countries military manual listed this rule according to IHL Database Customary Law, last modified April 27, 2020. https://ihl-databases.icrc.org/customary-ihl/eng/docs/v2_rul_rule10.
304) Formalized in Article 85(5) of the 1977 Additional Protocol I.

21. Massacare 1965(Indonesia Mass Killings of Communist Parties Member 1965-1966)

Key Point: The action of establishing an "opinion court" and its effect to resolve human right issue also is a big part of the history of Indonesia

1) Facts

In 1965, a group of military officers led by Lieutenant Colonel Untung kidnaped and assassinated Indonesia military high commanders[305)]. They were General Ahmad Yani, Lieutenant General Suprapto, Liuetenant General MT Haryono, Lietenant General Soeparman, Major General Sutoyo, Major General DI Pandjaitan and Captain Pier Tendean which their body found in Lubang Buaya Village[306)].

This created outrage in Indonesia that resulted in massive extra-judicial execution. Due to the illegal arrest of civilians by the authority of the Indonesia Communist Party (PKI), PKI was accused of the preparation of the kidnapping and assassination[307)].

Some activists and survivors held an "opinion court". In November 10 to 13 of 2015 in Den Haag Netherland, International Peoples Tribunal (IPT) 1965 was held.

2) IPT report

According to the final report of IPT 1965 especially in C Part of Finding and Recommendation, it was stated that government is responsible for Crimes against Humanity in this case because the government purged Indonesia Communist Party (Partai Komunis Indonesia: PKI). The

305) Komisi untuk Orang Hilang dan Korban Tindak Kekerasan, *Menyusun Puzzle Pelanggaran HAM 1965: Sebuah Upaya Pendokumentasian,* Jakarta: KontraS, 2012, p.7.

306) Tentara Nasional Indonesia, *Buku Panduan Monumen Pancasila Sakti*, Jakarta: Mabes TNI, 2008, p. 64.

307) Komisi untuk Orang Hilang dan Korban Tindak Kekerasan, *Op.cit,* p.8.

military created false information and false propaganda that caused the purge. During the false allegation and accession, PKI leaders, members, supporters, their families were staged under the chain of command[308].

There are many incidents that can fulfill the condition of the Crimes against Humanity in the purge[309]:

(1) Killing, a mass murder killing between 400 to 500.000[310]. This is stated in evidence B3 section (a)[311]. The widespread brutal and mass murder that happens in Indonesia constitutes crimes against humanity under the Rome Statute and violation of Indonesia criminal code article 138 and 140 and Law No. 26/2000[312];

(2) Imprisonment, At least 600,000 persons were imprisoned according to evidence B3 section (b) without justifiable reason.[313] It is a violation of Law No. 26/2000[314];

(3) Enslavement, There were evidences that imprisoned persons were forced to work in accordance with evidence B3 section (c).[315] This is a crime against humanity and violation of the 1930 convention concerning Forced or Compulsory Labour and Law No. 26/2000[316];

(4) Torture, Considerable documents have shown that torture is widely used in accidents proven by evidence B3 Section (d).[317] Torture is explicitly forbidden under Indonesia constitution law especially 28g(2) and Law No. 39/1999 on Human Rights and absolutely

308) International People Tribunal 1965 Final Report Findings and Documents of the International People's Tribunal on Crimes against Humanity Indonesia 1965 Chapter C. C1 Finding, p.83-86.
309) *Ibid.*
310) This number is not clear due to the non-disclosure policy of national secrets until 2020.
311) IPT 1965 report of Judge, p.36.
312) *Ibid,* p.39.
313) *Ibid,* p.40.
314) *Ibid.* p.43.
315) *Ibid.*
316) *Ibid.* p.45.
317) *Ibid.*

baned Internationally[318];

(5) Enforced disappearance, evidence B3 Section (e) shows that enforced disappearance started with Imprisonment and execution from the Indonesia Human Right Commission Report[319];

(6) Sexual violence, the evidence in B4 of the decision and the Woman Right Commission with Sexual Violence shows that systematic and massive sexual violence aiming at women who allegedly a communist party supporter was committed.[320] It is against Indonesia Law No. 26/2000[321];

(7) Exile, many Indonesian abroad involuntarily lost their right to citizenship while staying abroad and force them into exile status in accordance with evidence B5[322];

(8) Propaganda, evidence B6 shows the three-decade-long propaganda that alters what happens in 1965 and Government justification of what happened in 1965 and continuity of prosecution of the victim and family[323];

(9) Complicity, with another country like the US, Australia and the UK had their share in the accident according to evidence B7[324];

(10) Genocide, according to evidence B8 shows that the purge is aimed at certain "Indonesia Nation Group"[325] that concurrent with genocide definition in 1948 Genocide Convention which Indonesia is bound[326].

With these reasons, the Judge Recommended that[327]:

318) *Ibid.* p.46.
319) *Ibid.* p.47.
320) *Ibid.* p.49.
321) *Ibid.* p.52.
322) *Ibid.* p.53.
323) *Ibid.* p.56.
324) *Ibid.* p.62.
325) *Ibid.* p.72.
326) *Ibid.* p.73.
327) *Ibid.*

(1) Apologize to the victims and their family by the government of Indonesia;

(2) Investigate and prosecute all crimes against humanity;

(3) Ensure appropriate compensation for the victim and their family.

3) Comments

(1) The Role of International People Tribunal

Joshua Oppenheimer's movie the Act of Killing (2012) and the Look of Silence (2014) gave the international impact of how the Indonesian military had pre-planned and committed an act of inhume and cruelty[328)]during the incident in 1965. One of the international community's actions to find and judge this case is International People Tribunal 1965(IPT 1965) in 2015. IPT 1965 cannot be considered as a "legal court" such as the International Court of Justice (ICJ) or The International Criminal Court (ICC). It is not a mandated crime court that ensures justice or compensation for the victim or victim's family, but it is a court that will endeavor and push state responsibility for the victim and its family[329)]. When the International People Tribunal more serves as an "opinion court", it is nothing new in the International legal community. One of them is the Permanent People Tribunal in Italy which is built from the spirit to "give recognition, visibility. It voiced the people suffering from their fundamental right"[330)]. Furthermore, the initiator Lelio Basso said that[331)]:

"The dictates of public conscience can become a recognized source

328) Oki Rahadianto Sutopo, *The Act of Killing and The Look of Silence: A critical reflection*, Crime Media Culture, February 2017, p.3. last modified April 5, 2020, https://www.researchgate.net/publication/317137214_The_Act_of_Killing_and_The_Look_of_Silence_A_critical_reflection_2017/link/5c46d4ce458515a4c7377dd9/download.

329) International People Tribunal 1965 Press Release April 16, 2016, last modified April 5, 2020, https://www.tribunal1965.org/en/international-peoples-tribunal-ipt-1965/

330) See Permanent People Tribunal, on the website: http://permanentpeoplestribunal.org/?lang=en.

331) *Ibid.*

> of law and a tribunal emanating directly from the conscience of the people reflects an idea that is bound to grow. It is claimed that institutions derive their power from the people, but these two have moved further and further apart and only a major public initiative can try to build a bridge between the people and power".

People Tribunal aims is to create pressure or bridge from the people to either government or international legal institution to take serious action on certain cases.

(2) Genocide

Before World War II, the term "genocide" is not used as a single source of crime. Genocide is included in a Crime against Humanity or Extermination. An example of this case can be found in International Military Tribunal for the Far East Special proclamation by the supreme commander for the Allied Powers at Tokyo on January 19, 1946. Tribunal was established on January 19, 1946. Section II on Jurisdiction and General Provision includes the definition of 'Crimes Against Humanity' as[332)]:

> "murder, extermination, enslavement, deportation, and other inhumane acts committed against any civilian population, before or during the war, or persecutions on political or racial grounds in the execution of or in connection with any crime within the jurisdiction of the Tribunal, whether or not in violation of the domestic law of the country where perpetrated Leaders."
>
> "Organizers, instigators and accomplices participating in the formulation or execution of a common plan or conspiracy to commit any or the foregoing crimes are responsible for all acts performed by any person in execution of such plan."

332) Charter dated January 19, 1946; amended charter dated April 26, 1946.

Terms of Genocide at first used in Raphael Lemkin's book "the Axis Rule In Occupied Europe".[333] Lemkin introduced Genocide as a word combining *'genos'*(Greek word for people or race) and *'cide'(*Latin word for an act of killing), which he described the word as the destruction of a nation or ethnic group.[334] After the word was introduced, this word then was used in international conventions such as the Convention on the Prevention and Punishment of the Crime of Genocide 1948. Article II of Convention on the Prevention and Punishment of the Crime of Genocide 1948 states that:

> "In the present Convention, genocide means any of the following acts committed with intent to destroy, in whole or in part, a national, ethnical, racial or religious group, as such : (a) Killing members of the group; (b) Causing serious bodily or mental harm to members of the group; (c) Deliberately inflicting on the group conditions of life calculated to bring about its physical destruction in whole or in part; (d) Imposing measures intended to prevent births within the group; (e) Forcibly transferring children of the group to another group."

333) Lemkin Raphael, *Axis Rule In Occupied Europe*, Concord: Ramford Press 1944, p.123.
334) *Ibid.*

22. Aceh Conflict Resolution 1979(Free Aceh Movement "Gerakan Aceh Merdeka/GAM")

Key Point: Alternative conflict resolution model regarding Non-International armed conflict was used at Aceh Conflict

1) Facts

Many separatist groups aim to create their state in Indonesia. Indonesia Islamic State (Negara Islam Indonesia: NII), Republic of South Mollucas (Republik Maluku Selatan: RMS), Free Aceh Movement (Gerakan Aceh Merdeka: GAM) are examples of it. The reason behind this separatist action varies. Some ask for freedom, some think the government has been unfair to them, some with ideology reason, political and many more have been found in the history of separatism in Indonesia.

According to the Indonesian criminal code, *Aanslag* (separatism) mean that "the attempt undertaken with the intent to bring the territory of the state wholly or partially under foreign domination or to separate part thereof shall be punished by life imprisonment or maximum imprisonment of twenty years"[335).

A separatist group of GAM aims to ensure the survivability of people of Aceh-Sumatra as a nation to save their political, social, cultural, and religious heritage which are being destroyed by the Javanese colonialists and to reopen "the question of decolonization of the Dutch East Indies alias 'Indonesia'"[336).

Indonesian government took a military operation between 1976 to1979 (the first step of Aceh armed separatism action) and the government made the leader either exiled, killed or imprisoned after winning over GAM(the

335) See Article 106 of Indonesia Criminal Code (Kitab Undang-Undang Hukum Pidana/KUHP).

336) Kirsten E Schulze, *The Free Aceh Movement (GAM): Anatomy of a Separatist Organization*, Washington: East-West Center Washington, p.20.

first GAM insurgency[337]).

After training in Libya from 1986, GAM launched a second separatism attempt and the government responded with Red Net (Jaring Merah) Operation between 1989 to1998 (Military Operation Area: Daerah Operasi Militer)[338]. The GAM conducted a third separatism attempt between 1998[339] to 2005. Helsinki Agreement (The Aceh Peace Agreement) was signed in 2001 and continues to strengthen the autonomy of the Aceh region.

2) Aceh Peace Agreement

Aceh insurgency and the Indonesian government signed a peace agreement on 15 August year 2005. Some of the crucial points in the agreement are:

(1) Mandates that Aceh will have a right of special right to control judiciary and public administration except for international relation and external defense, national security, monetary and fiscal matters, justice, and freedom of religion. Still, the policymaking power will belong to the Government of the Republic of Indonesia in conformity with the Constitution. All the international agreements or national legislation regarding Aceh should be consulted with Aceh local government. Furthermore, Aceh will be reviving Aceh Qanun law;

(2) Allow Aceh to have a local political party to compete in Aceh election;

(3) Allow Aceh to have a special economy right to regulate internal tax and retain seventy (70) percent of the revenues from all current and future hydrocarbon deposits and other natural resources in the

337) *Ibid*, p.18.
338) *Ibid.*
339) *Ibid.*

territory of Aceh as well as in the territorial sea surrounding Aceh;

(4) Establish a human right court and human right commission to investigate abuse committed during the conflict;

(5) Offer an amnesty to all persons who have participated in GAM activities as soon as possible;

(6) Call for GAM to disarm by the end of the year;

(7) Establish the Aceh Monitoring Mission (AMM) by the European Union and ASEAN contributing countries with the mandate to monitor the implementation of the commitments taken by the parties in this Agreement.

3) Comments

(1) Autonomy and Special Region in Indonesia

Aceh autonomy gave two implications for the internal and external relationship of Indonesia. For internal relations, the Aceh region is added to the special region such as Yogyakarta, Jakarta, Papua and West Papua. It is uncommon for a unilateral state like Indonesia to give special autonomy to its territory. However, Indonesian Constitution Art. 18b verse 1 states that[340]:

> "The State recognizes and respects units of regional authorities that are special and distinct, which shall be regulated by law"

And Verse 2 states that[341]:

> "The State recognizes and respects traditional communities along with their traditional customary rights as long as these remain in existence and are following the societal development and the principles of the Unitary State of the Republic of Indonesia, and shall be regulated by law."

340) See Article 18b verse 1 of Indonesia Constitution (Undang-Undang Dasar 1945).
341) See 18b Verse 2 of Indonesia Constitution (Undang-Undang Dasar 1945).

Indonesian constitution gave recognition to special territory within Indonesia as long as it is asymmetric with national law. Yogyakarta, for example, has a special region. First, the governor of Yogyakarta is not chosen by direct election. It is chosen by two Yogyakarta Royal lineages from Sultanate of Yogyakarta Sultan as the governor and Pakualaman Residence Pakualam as vice-governor. Second, Yogyakarta has a traditional land law and Traditional Land Notary department under the Sultanate of Yogyakarta called Panitikismo handles Sultanate owned land (Sultan Ground). Yogyakarta has four types of ownership of land (two private and two government-owned) that is i) Sultan Ground ii) Pakualaman ground iii) private-owned iv) government owned[342)]. Simply Yogyakarta is guaranteed to have a right to keep its traditional ways of Yogyakarta royalty.

Another case is Papua[343)]. The special autonomy for Papua is nearly the same as what Aceh has. Papua does not allow to have a local party like Aceh, but Papua has a unique government system that consisted of the existence of Papuan People Representative Council beside Regular Province People Council. Member of Papua People Representative Council has 1 quarter more member than the Province People Council[344)]. Another special status entitled to Papua is Papuan People Assembly (Majelis Rakyat Papua) [345)]. Also, the Papuan governor can be selected only from the direct descendant of the Papuan people[346)]. Another major advantage is the economic and socio-cultural advantage stipulated in Chapter IX and Chapter X. They are also entitled to tribe court in certain cases[347)].

342) Law No.13/2012 on Speciality of Region of Yogyakarta.
343) Law No.21/2001 on Special Otonomy for Papua Province.
344) See Article 6, Law No.21/2001 on Special Autonomy for Papua Province.
345) See Article 19, Law No.21/2001 on Special Autonomy for Papua Province.
346) See Article 12 verse 1, Law No.21/2001 on Special autonomy for Papua Province.
347) See Article 50 verse 2, Law No.21/2001 on Special autonomy for Papua Province.

(2) Conflict Resolution of Aceh

Article 33 of the United Nation Charter stated that[348]:

> "The parties to any dispute, the continuance of which is likely to endanger the maintenance of international peace and security, shall, first of all, seek a solution by negotiation, enquiry, mediation, conciliation, arbitration, judicial settlement, resort to regional agencies or arrangements, or other peaceful means of their own choice."

Art. 33 confirms peaceful method to be conducted before heading to the armed conflict. Jawahir Thontowi Explain that[349]:

> "Much of Indonesian legal experts disagree on the government step to resolve Aceh conflict using a goodwill functions of the Indonesian government. GAM made Indonesian people united, but Indonesia must accept, as GAM's wish granted by Indonesian government, it is not for just legal regulations and reasons, but functions and benefit for peace, disarmament, and monitoring. Helsinki MOU, is not just matter of law but much more important. The Helsinki MOU provided a model for conflicts resolution in ASEAN."

Furthermore, M. Nur Djuli, the former member of the negotiating team for the GAM said that Helsinki MOU is one of the successful peace resolutions. Even country outside ASEAN like Afganistan visited Aceh to learn about Aceh Peace Process and many ex-negotiation teams from Indonesian government and GAM regularly are invited to talk and discuss it around the world[350].

348) Article 33 UN Charter.

349) Live Interview with Jawahir Thontowi by the Writer on October 16, 2019 Via Whatssapp Video Call.

350) M. Nur Djuli, *Aceh Peace Process: Revisiting 'White Helsinki'*, February 22, 2018. last modified october 20, 2019 https://www.thejakartapost.com/academia/2018/02/22/aceh-peace-process-revisiting-white-helsinki.html.

23. Indonesia Reformation 1998

Key point: Forced disappearance citizen cases during a mass demonstration in 1998 is a problem half-solved

1) Facts

In 1998, multi-element of the social group gathered in a massive demonstration with an intention to bring down President Soeharto (2nd President). This social justice movement is called 'reformation 1998[351]. In this demonstration, a case of kidnapping and torture was committed by security forces[352]. This condition was intensified with the economic crisis in 1997 resulted in 2,244 dead bodies (mostly burned), 91 injured and 31 people missing. A team of volunteers for humanitarian organizations reported that most of the victims were ordinary people[353].

2) Court Decision

There is only one court decision regarding reformation 1998. The military elite unit called Rose Team was pointed to blame for the missing activist personal between 1997 to 1998 and they have been brought to the military court. In the Indonesia Military Court decision PUT.25-16/K-AD/MMT-II/IV/1999, some member of Rose Team was found guilty and being punished[354]. Among defendant who was sent to an appeal, some were

---

351) Junge J. Fabian, *Indonesia: Kesempatan yang Hilang, Janji yang tak Terpenuhi : Pengadilan Ham Ad Hoc Kejahatan di Tandjung Priok*, Jakarta: Kontras/Watch Indonesia, 2008, p.7.

352) Singh, Biver, *Succession Politics in Indonesia -The 1998 Presidential Elections and the Fall of Suharto*, London: McMillan Press Ltd 2000, p.82.

353) Bourchier, David and Hadiz, Vedi, *Indonesian Politics and Society: A Reader*, London and New York: Rotledge Curzon, p.292.

354) Kontras, (Siaran Pers: Klarifikasi dan Informasi tentang Proses Pengadilan Tim Mawar) Press release: Clarification and Information about Rose Team Trial. 1)Major Inf Bambang Kristiono (Rose Team Commander) – Jailed for 1 year 10 Month and fired from Indonesia Armed Forces (Indonesia Army Branch); 2) Captain Inf Fausani Syahrial Multhazar (Rose Team Vice Commander) – Jailed for 1 year and 8 Month Fired From Indonesia Armed Forces

promoted and still in a strategic position in the military[355].

3) Comments

(1) Force Disappearance

Rome statute 1998 defines force disappearance as[356]:

> "Enforced disappearance of persons" means the arrest, detention or abduction of persons by, or with the authorization, support or acquiescence of, a State or a political organization, followed by a refusal to acknowledge that deprivation of freedom or to give information on the fate or whereabouts of those persons, to remove them from the protection of the law for a prolonged period of time."

It qualifies as a crime against humanity[357]. In article 2 of the International Convention for the Protection of All Persons from Enforced Disappearance 2006, force disappearance is[358]:

> "For the purposes of this Convention, "enforced disappearance" is considered to be the arrest, detention, abduction or any other form of

(Indonesia Army Brach); 3) Captain Inf Nugroho Sulistiyo Budi - Jailed for 1 year 8 Month and Fired From Indonesia Armed Forces (Indonesia Army Branch); 4) Captain Inf Yuius Selvanus – Jailed for 1 year 8 Month and Fired From Indonesia Armed Forces (Indonesia Army Branch); 5) Captain Inf Untung Budi Harto – Jailed 1 year and 8 Month Fired From Indonesia Armed Forces (Indonesia Army Branch); 6) Captain Inf Dadang Hendra Yuda – Jailed 1 year 4 Month (Indonesia Army Brach); 7) Captain Inf Djaka Budi Utama – Jailed 1 Year 4 Month (Indonesia Army Branch); 8) Captain Inf Fauka Noor Farid – Jailed 1 Year and 4 Month; 9) Master Sargeant Sunaryo- Jailed 1 Year; 10) Master Sergeant Sigit Sugianto- Jailed 1 Year; 11) First Class Sergeant Sukadi- Jailed 1 Year.

355) *Ibid;* 1) Lieutenant Colonel. Fausani Syahrial Multhazar, Commander of Military District Commando 0719 Jepara; 2) Lieutenant Colonel. Untung Budi Harto, Commander of Military District Commando 1504 Ambon; 3) Lieutenant Colonel. Dadang Hendra Yuda, Commander of Military District Commando 0801 Pacitan; 4) Lieutenant Colonel. Djaka Budi Utama, Commander of Infantry Batallion 115 Macan Lauser.

356) Rome Statute Article 7.2(i).

357) Article 7.1(i) of Rome Statute.

358) Article 2 of International Convention for the Protection of All Persons from Enforced Disappearance 2006.

deprivation of liberty by agents of the State or by persons or groups of persons acting with the authorization, support or acquiescence of the State, followed by a refusal to acknowledge the deprivation of liberty or by concealment of the fate or whereabouts of the disappeared person, which place such a person outside the protection of the law."

The text of Article 2 (of the ECHR 1950) read as a whole, demonstrates that it covers not only intentional killing but also the situations where it is permitted to use force which may result, as an unintended outcome, in the deprivation of life. Article 2 may also imply in certain well-defined circumstances a positive obligation on the authorities to take preventive operational measures to protect an individual for whom they are responsible.

24. Sampit Conflict 2001

Key Point: Peace Settlement of Ethnics Conflict on different moral values and customary "adat" values was conducted with efforts of the government entity

1) Facts

In February 2001, Dayaks indigenous groups (indigenous people of Borneo/Kalimantan island) and Madurese ethnics groups (transmigrants ethnics from the Madura island) clashed in a massive strike in the city of Sampit, Pontianak-Central Kalimantan Province[359]. Indonesian people recognized this massive clash as a "Sampit Conflict". As a result of this incident, deaths on the Madurese side reached as many as 500 besides displacement of 100,000[360], and material loss of burned 1992 houses, 16 cars, 43 Motorcycles, 114 pedicabs. The loss on the Dayaks side is unconfirmed. The history of sporadic violence goes back to 1950 and lasted multidecade.

In April 2001, Komnas HAM (Indonesian National Commission of Human Rights) approved the establishment of a commission of inquiry to investigate serious ethnic clash in Kalimantan through Komnas HAM decision SK No. 24/KOMNAS HAM/V/2001. The investigation team for the "Sampit conflict" analyzed the ethnic clashes whit a gross human right violation base on the criteria set in Law No. 26/2000 on Human Rights Court[361]. The team tried to find alternative ways to achieve peace and reconciliation and examined the role of state forces as well as other groups. The team gathered materials and perpetrated during and after the ethnics clashes in Sampit. The team found that weak internal police

359) There were 17 criminal cases, with the parties are between Dayaks and Mudarese since 1982. This incident is known as the beheading of Madurese by Dayaks.

360) See Sampit Conflict in Wikipedia, website: https://id.wikipedia.org/wiki/Konflik_Sampit.

361) Criteria of gross human rights violation stated in article 7,8, and 9 of Law No. 26/2000 on Human Rights Court.

coordination contributed to the social factors which led to the violence and found no evidence of a widespread systematic attack on the civilian population by either ethnic group. Therefore, the team reported that there was no gross violation of human rights as defined in article 9 of Law No. 26/2000 on Human Rights Court[362].

2) Sampit Settlement

No court decision came out concerning the Sampit conflict because the Komnas HAM didn't find any human rights violation although there are hundreds of dead, thousands of injured and material losses caused by the conflict. The government had worked to settle the conflict between Dayaks and Madurese by peaceful means. Several steps have taken by the government for local society. Actions of normalization, consolidation and stabilization have been adopted, such as:

(1) Local-level: involving local government, community leaders, religious/traditional leaders, youth leaders and security officials;

(2) Regional level: involving 4 Kalimantan governors (South, Central, West and East Kalimantan);

(3) National Level: involving two dispute ethnics (Dayaks and Madurese) with a government as the facilitator, this national meeting is called "Tekad Damai Anak Bangsa";

(4) Indonesian president meeting started with Abdurahman Wahid (4th Indonesia President) and continued with Megawati Soekarno Putri (5th Indonesia president) to support indigenous tribes to strengthen ties of adat/custom with principles "Semangat Rumah Betang".

Based on the result of the Central Kalimantan People's Congress, which took place on 4-7 June 2001 in Palangkaraya, the two conflicting parties

362) Horst Ficher, *Year Book of International Humanitarian Law,* Vol.4, 2001, p.539.

agreed on the following settlement:

(1) Accept the invitation to peace and apology from the citizens of Madura to Kalimantan indigenous people (Dayaks);

(2) Forgive the other party. If the two parties have forgiven each other and are determined to live side by side in peace, then the steps for re-evacuation, rehabilitation and law enforcement can be carried out in accordance with regulations;

(3) Return to Madurese. Those who will return to Central Kalimantan must undergo selection and the conditions are regulated in regional regulations regarding population;

(4) Bear in mind that the re-evacuation process must be carried out through negotiations, mental readiness from both parties, then sufficient cooling periods are still needed until the situation and mental condition of both parties are able to introspect themselves to achieve harmony.

3) Comments

(1) Human Rights Breach

Sampit conflict is a conflict between tribes on a large scale that resulted in fatalities of more than 500 death of ethnic Dayaks and Madurese. It began with several incidents committed by individuals and small groups between dayaks and madurese in several cities in the west and central of Kalimantan, after that in 2001 it became a massive clash between dayaks and madurase by linking the old incident and several criminal acts in the past.

After the conflict, a public issue of sampit conflict became an issue of a human right violation. That is why a Komnas HAM (Indonesian National Commission of Human Rights) has established a commission of inquiry to investigate the sampit conflict by Law No. 26/2000 on Human Rights

Court. Definition of genocide and crimes against humanity are applied at Law No. 26/2000 on Human Rights Court.

The Komnas HAM did not find any human rights violation during the investigation. Some of the pieces of evidence are however pointing the criteria of genocide[363)] of Art. 8, especially, the killing of ethnic aspect has found, which stated:

(1) Ethnic aspect: Dayaks as indigenous people of Kalimantan/Borneo island and Madurese as trans-migrant ethnics from Madura island;
(2) Ethnic Dayaks and Madurese are civilians;
(3) Acts of murder to members of ethnic groups (Dayak or Madura) on a large scale on the basis of ethnic equation (for Dayaks and Madurese) between Dayak and Madura tribes when the Sampit conflict occurs.

It was also difficult to find pieces of evidence enough to prove crimes against humanity[364)] committed by dayaks and/or madurese up to the level of investigation by the Indonesian National Human Rights Commission. First, responsible figures in both ethnic groups are absent. Second, Sampit conflict occurred in the form of anger accompanied by acts of resistance

363) Article 8 Law No. 26 of 2000 on Human Rights Court: "The crime of genocide is any act committed with the intent to destroy or destroy all or part of a nation, race, ethnic group, religious group, by (a) Killing group members; (b) cause severe physical or mental suffering to group members; (c) creating conditions for group life which will result in physical destruction in whole or in part; (d) enforcing actions aimed at preventing birth within the group or forcibly transferring children from one group to another".

364) Article 9 Law No. 26 of 2000 on Human Rights Court: "Crime against humanity is an act carried out as part of a widespread or systematic attack which is known to be directed against a civilian population, in the form of (a) murder; (b) annihilation; (c) slavery; (d) forced eviction or resettlement of residents; (e) arbitrary deprivation of liberty or other physical freedom that violates the basic principles of international law; (f) torture; (g) rape, sexual slavery, forced prostitution, forced coercion, forced infertility or sterilization or other forms of equal sexual violence; (h) the persecution of a certain group or association based on equality of political, racial, nationality, ethnicity, culture, religion, gender or other reasons that have been universally recognized as prohibited under international law; (i) enforced disappearances; or (j) apartheid crimes".

and self-defense of the indigenous people against the immigrant ethnics group (Madurese) triggered by a group of criminal acts committed by Madurese towards Dayaks. Third, when the Sampit conflict occurs in Feb 2001, the action taken by Madurese is an act of defending themselves from the action taken by the ethnic group Dayaks at that time.

The Sampit conflict is a conflict that occurs due to the different moral values and customary "adat" values. The result of the Sampit conflict was peace between the two ethnics that was quarreled by the government as a facilitator and ending up establishing the 2015 Dayak-Madura Sampit Peace Monument in Sampit-Central Kalimantan.

25. Bali Bombing 2002

Key Point: Indonesia Anti-Terrorism Law was enacted Retroactively after Bali bombing 2002

1) Facts

On October 12, 2002, the Bali bombing tragedy happened. Three bombs blasted simultaneously at different locations at 23:05 WITA. The first explosion occurred at Paddy's Pub Irish Pub using TNT (*Trinitrotoluene*) by the ISA with a suicide bomb vest. The second explosion occurred at 23:05 WITA +5 seconds near the Sari Club using an Ammonium Nitrate explosive that was placed inside the Mitsubishi L300 car driven by Jimi as Suicide Bomber. The last explosion occurred at 23:06 WITA + 5 seconds near the United States consulate in Denpasar using TNT explosives.

The victims of the Bali bomb blast reached 202 people consisting of 88 Australians, 38 Indonesians, 23 Britains, 7 Americans, 6 Germans, 5 Swedish citizens, 4 Dutch citizens, 3 France residents, 3 Danish citizens, 3 Swiss citizens, 2 New Zealanders, 2 Brazilian citizens, 2 Canadians, 2 Japanese citizens, 2 South Africans, 2 South Koreans, 1 Ecuadorian citizen, 1 Greek citizen, 1 Irish citizen, 1 Italian citizen, 1 Polish citizen, 1 Portuguese, 1 citizen 1, and 2 foreign citizens whose citizenship is unknown.

There are 26 suspects of Bali Bomb I blast[365)] and six main suspects are Amrozi, Ali Imron, Ali Gufhron, Imam Samudra, Dr. Azahari Husin and Dulmatin[366)].

---

365) The 26 suspects of Bali Bombing 1: (1). Amrozi Bin Nurhasyim; (2). Ali Imron "*Amrozi's younger brother's*"; (3). Ali Ghufron or Muklas, "*Amrozi's brothers*"; (4). Arnasan alias Jimi, as a sucide bomber's; (5). Imam Samudra or Abdul Aziz; (6). Abdul Gani; (7). Abdul Hamid; (8). Abdul Rauf; (9). Achmad; (10). Andi Hidayat; (11). Andi Oktavia; (12). Bambang Setiono; (13). Budi Wibowo; (14). Dr. Azahari Husin; (15). Dulmatin; (16). Ferry iqbal or isa; (17). Herlambang; (18). Hernianto; (19). Indris or Jonhi Hendrawan; (20) Junaedil; (21). Makmuri; (22). Mohammad Musafak; (23). Mohammad Najib Nawawi; (24). Umar Patek; (25). Mubarok Alias Utomo Pamungkas; (26). Zulkarnaen.

366) The exact detailed decision can't be founded but only the case number and the main decision can be accessed by the public.

2) Court Decision

26 suspects were prosecuted and four of them were brought to justice. Three of them have received a death sentence and one suspect has received life imprisonment. At the district level, Amrozi was prosecuted by the public prosecutor on June 30, 2003, and sentenced to death on July 7, 2003. Then amrozi submitted a Judicial Review as many as 3 times to the Supreme Court but all were rejected by the Supreme Court.

Then with a different case number, the defendant Imam Samudra was prosecuted by the public prosecutor on July 28, 2003, and sentenced to death on September 10, 2003. Ali Gufron received a death sentence by the public prosecutor on August 28, 2003, and was sentenced to death on October 2, 2003. The three defendants of Amrozi, Ali Gufron and Imam Samudra received death sentences, while Ali Imron, in a different court proceeding, was sentenced to life imprisonment because Ali Imron was co-operative during the process. Suspect Dr. Azahari Husin was killed during a police ambush on November 9, 2005. Dulmatin at that time was a fugitive until 2010 was killed in a police ambush on March 9, 2010.

3) Comments

(1) Retroactive Principle

Before the Bali bombing 1, Indonesia did not have regulations on Anti-Terrorism. Although a draft of an anti-terrorism bill was introduced twice from 1990 until 2002 the design of the anti-terrorism law has not yet reached the result. The Bali bombing 1 occurred on October 12, 2002. At that time, the Indonesian state still did not have anti-terrorism law, then on October 18, 2002, the Indonesian president (then led by Megawati Soekarno Putri 5th Indonesia president) signed a government regulation to replace the Act Law (Perppu) No. 1/2002 on the Eradication of Terrorism and Government Regulations in lieu of Law (Perppu) No. 2/2002 on the enactment of Perppu No. 1/2002 concerning eradicating criminal acts of terrorism.

The Bali Bombers 1 was charged and tried using Perppu No. 1/2002 on the Eradication of Terrorism Crimes. Then on April 4, 2003. Perppu No. 1/ 2002 has passed into the Anti-Terrorism Law No. 15/2003. The Perppu No. 1/2002 has been applied retroactively and it conflicts with the principle of non-retroactivity.

Based on Art.1 verses (1) of the Indonesian Criminal Code, in principle, the law can only be applied to action after the law was adopted[367). However, Article 46 of Perppu No. 1/2002 makes it clear that the regulation can apply retroactively[368). So, the non-retroactive principle in the Indonesian Criminal Code is contrary to Perppu No. 1 of 2002 which applies the retroactive principle. If it is further understood, the application of the retroactive principle in Perppu No. 1/2002 is enforced because of the Bali bombing tragedy.

(2) Terrorism Punishment

Amrozi, Imam Samudra and Ali Gufron received the death penalty, the highest sentence in Perppu No. 1/2002 which later became Law No. 15/2003 concerning Anti-Terrorism for acts of the bombing. The Bali Bombing tragedy 1 was categorized as an act of Terrorism according to Perppu No. 1/2002 and Law No. 15/2003. Based on Perppu No. 1/2002, terrorism crimes is described as a threat to national security. Law No.15/2003 states that terrorism is an extraordinary crime result in casualties for Indonesian and foreign countries.

The death penalty should be sentenced with special consideration

367) Article 1 verses 1 of Indonesia Criminal Code: "An act cannot be convicted, except based on the strength of existing criminal law provisions".

368) Article 46 Perppu No. 1/2002: "Provisions in the Government Regulation in Lieu of this Act may be retroacted for legal action in certain cases before the entry into force of the Government Regulation in Lieu of this Law, the application of which is determined by Act or Government Regulation in lieu of a separate Act".

following due process. The death penalty aims to provide a deterrent effect to the perpetrators or potential perpetrators of criminal acts of terrorism. Although theoretically, the death penalty provides a crime deterrent effect to the citizen of that country, after the Bali bombing tragedy, various bombings also have occurred in the following years.

26. Death Sentence for the International Drug Traffickers 2005

Key Principle: Death Penalty punishment applies to drug traffickers in Indonesia

1) Facts

The death sentence has been given to the accused who committed serious crimes and drug trafficking. Drug crime has become a transnational crime committed without borders and regions. Indonesia has ratified the International Conventions on Narcotics and Psychotropics which have been implemented into Law No. 35/2009 on Narcotics. In this convention, Indonesia has recognized narcotics crimes as serious Crimes against Humanity, so their enforcement requires special, effective treatment and maxim sentence.

The death penalty for drug traffickers is regulated in Art. 113 paragraph (2), Art. 114 paragraph (2), Art. 118 paragraph (2), Art. 119 paragraph (2), Art. 121 paragraph (2) and Art. 114 paragraph (2) of the Law No. 35/2009 on Narcotics[369)]. Indonesia applies the principle of territoriality and domestic laws apply to both citizen and foreign nationals residing in the territory of the Republic of Indonesia. The death sentence can be given after making a good judgment based on sufficient evidence supporting the facts and legal analysis at the trial. Andrew Chen, who is an Australian citizen, was tried for a narcotic crime and sentenced to death.

2) Court Decision

Denpasar District Court in case No. 624/Pid.B/2005/ PN.Dps stated that[370)]:

369) The criminal provisions in Law No. 35/2009 on Narcotics.
370) Judial Review No. 37 PK/Pid.Sus/2011.

(1) Defendant Andrew Chan was proven guilty of committing criminal acts without rights and against the law of exporting narcotics Level 1;

(2) Criminal defendant gets capital punishment;

(3) The defendant to remain in custody until the final verdict in this case.

The defendant appealed to Denpasar High Court. The High Court of Denpasar No. 18/Pid.B/2006/PT.Dps Decided that[371]:

(1) Accept appeal to Denpasar High Court;

(2) Reinforce Denpasar District Court Decision No. 624/Pid.B/2005/PN.Dps.

In cassation, the defendant applied to the Supreme Court of Indonesia and the Supreme Court decision No. 1690 K/Pid/2006 rejected the cassation[372]. Then Defendant asked for a Judicial Review. No. 37 PK/Pid.Sus/2011 Judicial Review by the Indonesian Supreme Court Decision stated that[373]:

(1) Reject a request for Judicial Review from applicant Andrew Chan;

(2) The death penalty is upheld.

3) Comments

(1) Narcotics as Serious Crime

The urgency of the dangers of drugs in Indonesia based on a survey conducted by the National Narcotics Agency (BNN) and the Indonesian Institute of Sciences (LIPI) showed 2.3 million students in Indonesia had consumed narcotics. That figure is equivalent to 3.2 percent of the group's population. Drug use among students is also a problem on a global scale. World Drugs Reports 2018 from the United Nations Office on Drugs

371) *Ibid.*
372) *Ibid.*
373) *Ibid.*

and Crime (UNODC) found 5.6 percent of the world's population or 275 million people in the age range 15 to 64 years had taken drugs at least once. That is why the Indonesian government emphasizes the regulation related to narcotics and narcotics distribution in Indonesia This is to avoid narcotics abuse, especially among young generations.

Drug crime cases are considered as the most serious crime in Indonesia considering the consequences of destroying the future of the nation's children. Therefore, the death penalty is given to drug criminals. However, several scholars in Indonesia believe that there is no positive correlation between the death penalty and the reduced level of drug crime in Indonesia. Instead, the study shows an increased number of people's use expending from users and dealers to the producers[374)].

(2) Death Sentence

The death sentence to drug dealers accords with Art.114 paragraph (2) of Law No. 35/2009. The writer believes that it does not violate human rights because the death sentence is imposed on the person who damaged and destroy the crowd. If he lives, then the greater destruction toward the country will happen. And the implementation of the death penalty for narcotics crimes does not contradict international conventions because killing one person is better than destroying the people due to his actions and actions. Drug traffickers can possibly destroy more human if one is still alive[375)].

The death penalty to drug traffickers in Indonesia raises two different sides of public opinion. In this case, both supporters and opponents of capital punishment based their opinions on normative and sociological reasons. The majority of the public, around 84.1%, agree with the death

374) Umar Anwar, "Penjatuhan Hukuman Mati bagi Bandar Narkoba ditinjau dari Aspek Hak Asasi Manusia", *Jurnal Legislasi Indonesia*, Vol.13, 2016, p.244.
375) Umar Anwar, *Op.Cit*, p.249.

sentence to drug crime. Pros agree to the punishment to those drug criminals damaging young generation believing the deterrent effect to the society that the death penalty has. Whereas for those who disagree, give a reason that the death penalty is the most severe punishment type. They believe in behavior change of the human and the death penalty is a barrier to human rights[376].

376) Agus Purnomo, "Hukuman Mati Bagi Tindak Pidana Narkoba di Indonesia: Perspektif Sosiologi Hukum, De Jure", *Jurnal Hukum dan Syariah*, Vol.8, 2016, p.19.

27. Aceh LGBT Case 2017

Key Principle: Aceh province adopted the practice of shariah as its legal code and the practice of cane although arguably can be an act of torture, dualism state citizen can only refer to International treaty when the country adopts it in domestic law

1) Facts

In March 2017, after receiving a complaint from local people, vigilantes raided a house in Aceh and two gay men got caught[377].

2) Court Decision

An Islamic Shariah court in Aceh province sentenced two gay men to 85 ashes of cane in public. Both waived their right to get the assistance of defense lawyers. The sentence has handed down base on Law No. 6/2014 on Jinayah Law that says, "anyone who did Jarimah[378], Liwath[379] is going to be treated with 'Uqubat Tázir[380][381]".

The religious code Qanun was adopted by the provisional government and Aceh representatives Council (Dewan Perwakilan Rakyat Aceh: DPRA) in September 2014. This is based on the Law No. 44/1999 on the Implementation of the Aceh Privilege, Law No. 18/2001 on Special Autonomy for Nanggroe Aceh Province as Nanggroe Aceh Darussalam, Law. No. 11/2006 on Aceh Government, Law No. 48/2007 on the Stipulation of Government Regulation

377) 18&19/JN/2017/Ms.Bna.

378) Jarimah is an act prohibited by Sharia Islam. Jarimah is punished based on the Art 1, No. 16 of Qanun Aceh on Jinayat Law and No. 6 Act of Parliament 2014.

379) Liwath is an act punished based on the Art. 1 No. 28 of Qanun Aceh on Jinayat Law and No. 6 Law of Parliament 2014.

380) Uqubat is a sentence or punishment given by a judge to the perpetrator of Jarimah. Law. 1 No. 17 of Qanun Aceh on Jinayat Law and No. 6 Law of Parliament, 2014.

381) Tázir is a type of 'Uqubat that has been determined in Qanun that is the form of preference and it is measured in its highest and lowest limit. Act 1 no 19 of Qanun on Jinayat Law. The maximum punishment is 100 lashes of cane or a maximum fine of 1000 grams of pure gold or 100 months in prison. For repeat offenders will get another 100 lashes or 120 grams of pure gold and/or a sentence of a maximum of 12 months.

in lieu of law as replacement of Law No. 2/2007 on the management of legal problem for the implementation of rehabilitation and reconstruction area and people's lives in Nanggroe Aceh Darussalam Province and Nias Island North Sumatra[382].

3) Comments

(1) Pluralism

Indonesia is a country of legal pluralism[383]. Constitutional Court (Mahkamah Konstitusi) also declared that Islamic law is only one of the sources of law in Indonesia, alongside traditional customary law by indigenous people (Adat Law)[384], Islamic Law[385], civil law system with a strong influence of the Dutch and common law tradition[386].

John Griffith defines legal pluralism in his article as below.

"legal pluralism is a concomitant of social pluralism: the legal organization of society is congruent with its social organization. 'Legal pluralism' refers to the normative heterogeneity attendant upon the fact that social action always takes place in a context of multiple, overlapping, 'semi-autonomous social fields', which it may be added, is in practice a

382) Detailed explanation on the sharia contents is covered at Park Jihyun, Muhammad Tizar Adhiyatma, "Identification of Legal Pluralism in Indonesia and Republic of Korea", *Hanyang Journal of Law*, Vol.2, 2015, p.9.

383) Tim Lindsey and Mas Achmad Santosa, *The Trajectory of Law Reform in Indonesia: Short Overview of Legal Systems and Change in Indonesia*, in 「Tim Linsey Indonesia Law and Society」, 2nd Ed, The Federation Press, 2008, p.3.

384) *Adat* law governs the family system and *Adat* marriage. Also Law No. 5 of 1960 on Agrarian Law(Land law) is based on *Adat* Law.

385) Islamic law for Muslims which only governs matters concerning marriage, inheritance, succession, gifts, the endowment of money for religious purposes(*wakaf*), the giving of alms(-*shadagah*) and Islamic economic matters such as finance and banking. Reference laws are Presidential Instruction No. 1/1991 on the compilation of Islamic law, Islamic law(*Syariah*) of Law No. 3/2009 on the second amendment to Law No. 7/1989 on Religious Court Procedure.

386) For the overview of the Indonesian Legal System, please refer Rina Shahriyani Sharulla, Park Jihyun, "Implementation of International Treaty in Indonesia and Adoption of the Indonesian Court", *Yonsei Law Review*, Vol. 28 No.1, 2018, p.6; Ibid., p.27.

dynamic condition. A situation of legal pluralism -the omnipresent, normal situation in human society – is one in which law and legal institutions are not all subsumable within one 'system' but have their sources in the self-regulatory activities of all the multifarious social fields present, activities which may support, complement, ignore or frustrate one another, so that the 'law' which is actually effective on the 'ground floor' of society is the result of enormously complex and usually in practice unpredictable patterns of competition, interaction, negotiation, isolationism, and the like[387)]".

(2) Human Rights Aspect of LGBT Human

A human being is defined as a culture-bearing primate classified in the genus Homo, especially the species H. sapiens...human beings display a marked erectness of body carriage that frees the hands for use as manipulative members. Some of these characteristics, however, are not entirely unique to humans. The gap in cognition, as in anatomy, between humans and the great apes (orangutans, gorillas, chimpanzees, and bonobos) is much less than was once thought, as they have been shown to possess a variety of advanced cognitive abilities formerly believed to be restricted to humans[388)].

The rights inherited to humans have been listed or implied in many of the International conventions as well as resolutions in various UN committees. Not only that, but domestic laws are also designated to support the rights conferred to the citizen by the sovereign nation. However, international laws and domestic laws can be in conflict situations.

Countries that criminalize same-sex conduct are Algeria, Antigua & Barbuda, Bangladesh, Barbados, Bhutan, Brunei, Burundi, Cameroon, Chad, Comoros, Cook Islands, Dominica, Egypt, Eritrea, Eswatini,

387) John Griffiths, "What is legal pluralism, Journal of Legal Pluralism", *Journal of Legal Pluralism and Unofficial Law*, No.24, 1986, p.39.

388) Britannica Encyclopedia.

Ethiopia, Gambia, Ghana, Grenada, Guinea, Guyana, Iran, Jamaica, Kenya, Kiribati, Kuwait, Lebanon, Liberia, Libya, Malawi, Malaysia, Maldives, Mauritania, Mauritius, Morocco, Myanmar, Namibia, Nigeria, Occupied Palestinian Territory, Gaza Strip, Oman, Pakistan, Papua New Guinea, Qatar, Saint Kitts and Nevis, Saint Lucia, Saint Vincent and The Grenadines, Samoa, Saudi Arabia, Senegal, Sierra Leone, Singapore, Solomon Islands, Somalia, South Sudan, Sri Lanka, Sudan, Syria, Tanzania, Tonga, Tunisia, Turkmenistan, Tuvalu, Uganda, Uzbekistan, Yemen, Zambia, Zimbabwe[389)].

In South Korea, the military criminal code 92(6)(sexual molestation) punishes same-sex conduct with up to 2 years in prison[390)]. To defy discrimination, 'Discrimination Prohibition Law' has been proposed as a bill in 2007 and, 8th times before, again in 2020 to the 21st parliament. Even though LGBT are at the heart of the controversy, The 2020 survey showed that 87.7% of replier to the survey answered positively to the enactment of the 'Discrimination Prohibition Law' in Korea[391)].

In Indonesia, Aceh is the first province that practices Islamic law. Aceh approved and uses shariah as its legal code in addition to the national criminal code[392)]. After the implementation of Qanun Aceh No. 6/2014 on Jinayat Law, this is the first case that handed down a sentence[393)]. After this

389) Human Rights Watch, Type of Anti-LGBT Laws http://internap.hrw.org/features/features/lgbt_laws/.

390) The Military Criminal Code. After overturn of the "Conscientious objector to the military service" provision in the Constitution allowing alternative military service by the Constitutional Court, eliminating criminalization of soldier of LGBT became the hot issue. In 2018, in the case of a consensual sexual relationship of LGBT, the lower court reached the decision of not guilty.

391) News Prism, *14year frustration of non-passage of Discrimination Prohibition Law, will it be different this time?* (뉴스프리즘, 14년간 좌절된 차별금지법, 이번엔 통과될까?), Yonhapnewstv.co.kr, 05 July, 2020. https://www.yonhapnewstv.co.kr/news/MYH20200704007500038?did=1825m.

392) Arskal Salim & Azyumardi Azra, *Introduction in Sharia's and Politics in Modern Indonesia*, Arskal Salim & Azyumardi Azra eds. 2003.

393) For a detailed discussion on the laws applicable to LGBT in Aceh province refer Muhammad Tizar Adhiyatma, Park Jihyun, "The Verdict to Gay Couple in Aceh, is this Infringement of International Human Rights?", *Hanyang Journal of Law*, Vol.6, 2017.

2017 case, the Family Resilience Bill has introduced at the national level in 2020. This bill contains provisions that would force LGBTQ[394] people into government-sanctioned rehabilitation centers to "cure" them of their sexual orientation or gender identity[395].

Human Rights Watch called for the couple to be released immediately saying the punishment sought by prosecutors constitutes torture under International law[396]. For the purpose of Convention against Torture and Other Cruel, Inhuman or Degrading Treatment or Punishment[397]", the term "torture" means any act by which serve pain and suffering, whether physical or mental, is intentionally inflicted on a person for such purposes as obtaining from him or third person information or a confession, punishing him for an act he or a third person has committed or is suspected of having committed, or intimidating or coercing him or a third person, or for any reason based on discrimination of any kind, when such pain or suffering is inflicted by or at the instigation of or with the consent or acquiescence of a public official or other person acting in an official capacity. It does not include pain or suffering arising only from, inherent in or incidental to lawful sanction.[398]"

An act of punishment by the government punishing him/her for an act he/she has committed for any reason based on discrimination of any kind

394) LGBTQ is an acronym for Lesbian, Gay, Bisexual, Transgender and queer or questioning.

395) Nico Lang, *Indonesia Proposes Bill to Force LGBTQ people into 'Rehabilitation'*, NBC News, 3 March 2020. https://www.nbcnews.com/feature/nbc-out/indonesia-proposes-bill-force-lgbtq-people-rehabilitation-n1146861.

396) Adam Harvey, *Indonesian Prosecutors Demand Gay couple be Caned after Pleading Guilty in Sharia Court*, ABC News. 10, May 2017.

397) UNTS, vol 1465, p.85. Other conventions prohibiting torture are International Covenant on Civil and Political Rights: ICCPR Art.7, Art.10(1); Universal Declaration of Human Rights Art.5; the European Convention on Human Rights and Fundamental Freedom 1950 Art.3; the American Convention on Human Rights 1978 Art.5(2); the African Charter on Human and People's Rights 1981; the European Convention for the Prevention of Torture and Inhuman and Degrading Treatment or Punishment 1987; the Inter-American Convention to Prevention and Punishment 1985, etc.

398) G.A. Res. 39/46, U.N. GAOR, Supp. No. 51, pt. 1, art 1, at U.N. Doc. A/29/51(1984).

here for the reason of sexual orientation can be included in the definition of torture and therefore becomes a breach of obligation of treaty duty if a Member punishes the person.

However, there is also a domestic law applicable to the act of LGBT in Aceh province. Two different legal systems apply here. Which one prevails? Depends. It depends on the country which has taken a monism or dualism approach.[399)]

When the Supreme Court was asked to consider the legal validity of the *Qanun* Jinayat – the Aceh Criminal Code – which adopts aspects of Islamic criminal law and procedure, even though code provisions appear to violate human rights norms as reflected in international and Indonesian laws, the Supreme Court refused to hear the case, citing an unconvincing technicality[400)].

According to the UN between 0.05% and 1.7% of the global population are born with intersex traits[401)]. With these scientific statistics, the UN is moving toward eliminating discrimination based on the intersex. Germany had adopted third gender law in 2019 and does not require gender information mostly. Only passport document requires gender information.

399) Please read the ASEAN Charter-Constitutional Court Case for further discussion on the issue of monism and dualism.

400) Simon Butt, Religious Conservatism, "Islamic Criminal Law and the Judiciary in Indonesia: A Tale of Three Courts", *The Journal of Legal Pluralism and Unofficial Law*, Vol.50, 2018. p.402.

401) United Nations for LGBT EQUALITY fact sheet. The original document is attached. https://www.unfe.org/wp-content/uploads/2017/05/UNFE-Intersex.pdf.

28. Chandra and others v. Netherlands 2003

Key Principle: The interests of having a suitable place to live is not an issue of Article 8 of the European Convention on Human Rights

1) Facts

The European Court of Human Rights is a supranational court established by the European Convention on Human Rights[402]. It hears applications covering the breach of one or more of the human rights provisions concerning civil and political rights set out in the European Convention on Human Rights (ECHR) and its protocols by contracting states. An application can be lodged by an individual, a group of individuals or one or more of the other contracting states. The Court can either lender judgments or issue an advisory opinion[403].

A suit against the Deputy Minister of Justice of the Netherland, regarding a permit to stay for a family reunion was filed by the first applicant, Mrs. Roslina Chandra, a Netherlands national of Indonesian origin, born in 1958 and living in Eindhoven. The second, third, fourth and fifth applicantions were filed by Henry, Willian, Ayreen and Nivula Tjonadi, who are the first applicant's children, Indonesian nationals, born in 1979, 1980, 1983 and 1985, respectively. They currently live in Eindhoven with their mother[404].

In 1992, when the applicant (the mother) was in the process of getting divorced from her Indonesian husband (father of the other applicant). The reason for the divorce was frequent abuse of her and the children by her

402) European Commission, European Court of Human Rights (ECHR), last modified December 1, 2019 https://ec.europa.eu/home-affairs/what-we-do/networks/european_migration_network/glossary_search/european-court-human-rights-ecthr_en.

403) *Ibid.*

404) European Court of Human Rights, *Decision as to the Admissibility of Application no. 53102/99 by Roslina CHANDRA and Others against the Netherlands,* 13 May 2003, p.2.

husband. He also did not provide any basic daily needs and did not meet his responsibilities as a father.[405)] The father got custody of the children which remain with him until now, while the mother moves to the Netherland. The mother pursued a legal proceeding in the Netherlands for custody and finally granted it in April 1995. In July 1996, the mother obtained Netherlands Nationality and in January of 1977, the relationship between the mother and her partner in Netherland ended. Now she lives by herself.

Then in March 1997, the children of the mother entered the Netherlands on a short-stay visa. And on 12 May 1997, the children filed a formal application for a residence permit in order to stay with their mother in Netherland *(vergunning toot verbliif)*. However, it was rejected by the Deputy Minister of Justice because the criteria for a family reunion have not met upon the present application. The reason is first, the relation between the mother and the children is considered severed and second, the mother had an insufficient fund for living.

Thus, the children filed an objection to the decision by the Deputy Minister of Justice to the Hague Regional Court. However, the Regional Court also rejected the application by the applicant (The Children). The Regional Court saw no merit in the arguments, so the court refused the residence of the children. In this context, it had regarded facts that the proceedings concerned a request for the first admission to the Netherlands, rather than a refusal to extend existing residence. It further held that there were no objective obstacles to the applicant's family life being exercised elsewhere – the mother was free to develop family life with her children in Indonesia. The Regional Court stated that a proper balance had been struck between the interests of the applicants and those of society as a whole, the latter interest being served by a restrictive immigration policy[406)].

405) *Ibid.*
406) *Ibid*, p.3.

Hence, after going through the Regional Court of Hague, the applicant tried through the European Court of Human Rights Article 8 of the ECHR. They claimed that the residence in the Netherlands, for the purpose of family reunion, was refused to the children by the Netherlands authorities, and as a result of that, they could not enjoy family life with their mother[407].

2) Court Decision

Article 8 of the European Convention on Human Rights provides as follows:

(1) Everyone has the right to respect for his private and family life, his home and his correspondence;

(2) There shall be no interference by a public authority with the exercise of this right except such as is in accordance with the law and is necessary for a democratic society in the interests of national security, public safety, or the economic well-being of the country, for the prevention of disorder or crime, for the protection of health or morals, or for the protection of the rights and freedoms of others.

The Court is in the favor of the Government which mentioned that the Netherland authority's decision is not a violation of Article 8 of the convention. The Government was further of the opinion that no special facts or circumstances were there which would place them under a positive obligation to grant the children a residence permit. In this context, Government attached relevance, inter alia, to the fact that the mother had not applied for the children to be admitted to the Netherlands until 1997, that is five years after she had first arrived in the Netherlands. At that time, the mother made a conscious decision to settle in the Netherlands while leaving her children with their father. In addition, there is no one to care

407) Art 8 of European Convention on Human Rights.

for of children, in so far as they still are required such care: apart from their father, other relatives (siblings of their mother) and all caretakers ware also living in Indonesia.[408)]

The applicant argued that they have followed all the regulations including the immigration rules of the Netherland and mentioned that their mother already had several jobs in Netherland to fund their living expenses. Also, the mother's psychiatrist wrote a letter, dated 11 September 2001, saying that a return to Indonesia would lead to a deterioration of her situation, and a separation of mother and children would be harmful to both.

The Court reiterates that the essential object of Article 8 is to protect the individual from arbitrary action by the public authorities. There is an effective "respect" for family life. However, the boundaries between the State's positive and negative obligations under this provision do not lend themselves to precise definition. Although the Court appreciates that the applicants would now prefer to maintain and intensify their family life in the Netherlands, Article 8, as noted above, does not guarantee a right to choose the most suitable place to develop family life. Furthermore, Secondly, the applicants have failed to counter with a valid argument against advanced one by the Government to the effect that they might settle at a location in Indonesia away from the mother's ex-husband. For those reasons, the court by a majority declares that the application is inadmissible.

3) Comments

(1) Rights to Respect Private and Family life

Article 8 of the ECHR protects a person's right to respect for their

408) *Ibid,* p.6.

private and family life. Article 8 is a right that concerns an individual's need to live and develop in a social environment and to maintain relationships with others. Article 8 is a qualified right, which means that it can be interfered with by a public authority, such as the Home Office, in certain circumstances. Article 8(2) provides that:

> "There shall be no interference by a public authority with the exercise of this right except such as is in accordance with the law and is necessary for a democratic society in the interests of national security, public safety or the economic well-being of the country, for the prevention of disorder or crime, for the protection of health or morals, or for the protection of the rights and freedoms of others."

Immigration control is generally accepted to fall within the reasons specified in the convention. However, a public authority may only interfere with a person's right to respect for private and family life if the interference is proportionate. In this dispute, it is clear that the judge has rejected the plaintiff's claim because the plaintiff did not have a strong foundation and an overly private argument brought before the trial. Furthermore, the judge argued that in this case, the plaintiff could continue his life in Indonesia.

29. Mc.Donald House Bombing

Key Principle: Indiscriminate attacks on a civilian by the person who is not an active participant in combat can fall into the category of a war criminal even if the action was for the government

1) Facts

On March 10, 1965, a bomb exploded on a building on the orchard road of Singapore as part of Indonesia's confrontation with Malaysia from 1963 to 1966[409)]. A few months after the bombing incident, Singapore gained independence from Malaysia. This Mcdonald house bombing was part of the Indonesia government's "confrontation" policy to oppose the creation of the Malaysia federation from 1963 to 1966, and bomb attack killed 3 and injured 33 people.

Three days after the explosion, the two Indonesian marine commandos were caught as a suspect for the McDonald house bombing while escaping from Singapore by sea. They were rescued at sea by a bumboat man who saw them clinging to a plank. At that time, they were not wearing military uniforms and had no identification papers[410)]. They were later taken to a marine police boat and subsequently interrogated by the police before being charged with murder for their role in the MacDonald House bombing[411)].

According to the witness testimony at the trial, Bin Haji Mohamed Ali and Another v. Public Prosecutor said that he saw a Malayan Airways canvas traveling bag on the floor of the mezzanine floor. Smoke was coming from the bag and he heard a hissing noise. The explosion killed two

409) Insight Guides, *Insight Guides City Guide Singapore*, London: Apa Publications Group, 2016, p. 102.

410) Mohamed Effendy Abdul Hamid, *MacDonald House Bomb Explosion*, August 7, 2014, last modified March 19, 2020, https://eresources.nlb.gov.sg/infopedia/articles/SIP_62_2004-12-17.html.

411) *Ibid.*

secretaries employed by the bank and injured a driver who died two days later. Later examination of the building showed that the explosive used was 20 to 25 lbs pounds of *nitroglycerine*. On October 20, 1965, the appellants were convicted in the High Court of Singapore under the Penal Code of the murder for killing three civilians.

Then they have appealed to the Federal Court of Malaysia but the requests were dismissed on October 5, 1966[412]. Both men were hanged on 17 October 1968. This execution of the sentence spackled the attack of the Singapore embassy by around 400 Indonesia students while protesting the decision[413]. This incident made obstruction of bilateral relation between Indonesia and Singapore until 1973. In 1973, Singapore Prime Minister lee Kwan You went to Indonesia and scattered flower for those two in Kalibata Heroes Cemetary as a good gesture for Indonesia and Singapore relation[414] and the obstruction of two countries was solved.

2) Court Decision

The High Court of Singapore handed down a death sentence on October 20, 1965 after trying them with war crime. The accused appealed to the Federal Court of Malaysia. But the court led by Wee Chong Jin C.J., Tan Ah Tah and Ambrose JJ dismissed the appeal of the first appellant, Osman Bin Haji Mohamed Ali, and the second appeal of the appellant, Harun Bin Said alias Tahir. Then the accused appealed by special leave and but sentenced them to the death penalty by hanging[415].

The Judicial Committee of the Privy Council has examined international and national regulations. The Geneva Convention (III)(i. Relative to the Treatment of Prisoners of War; ii. 1950 Article 2 on Application; iii. Article

412) *Ibid.*
413) *Ibid.*
414) *Ibid.*
415) Appeal No.20 of 1967.

4 about Prisoners of war), Geneva Conventions Act, 1962[416] Section 4(1) on Notice, the Hague Convention (IV), its annex, regulations concerning the Laws and Customs of War on Land, 1907 (Article 1 on the status of belligerents, Article 29 on Spies and Article 31 about Spies).

The Judicial Committee of the Privy Council dismissed the appeal base on the argument that first, it is constitutional to use the 'emergency status' under the Malaysian Emergency Essential Power Act[417], Second, not every member of the Armed Forces when caught will be treated as a prisoner of war[418]. Prosecutor emphasized that international law recognizes the necessity of distinguishing between belligerents and peaceful inhabitants[419]. Base on the argument, the Judicial Committee refused to recognize the status of the prisoner of war for two appellants because the appellants were dressed in civilian clothes when committing sabotage when the place the explosives and lit them, and also at the time of their arrest[420].

3) Comments

(1) Qualification of Militia and Voluneer Corps

Historical background of this event is the confrontation between Indonesia and Malaysia. Indonesian president Soekarno did not agree to the formation of Malaysia[421]. At the time of confrontation, Singapore was still a part of Malaysia but when the final court decision came out, Singapore was Independent from Malaysia. Indonesian government objected to the establishment of Malaysia thinking that the role of Malaysia would be just

416) Malaysia Legislation on Ratification of Geneva Convention Relative To the Treatment Of Prisoners of War 1949.

417) Bin Haji Mohamed Ali and Another v. Public Prosecutor Judicial Committee of the Privy Council (U.K.), 29 July 1968, p.3.

418) *Ibid*, p.6.

419) *Ibid.*

420) *Ibid*, p.8.

421) Marsita Omar, Indonesia–Malaysia Confrontation, last modified March 19, 2020, https://eresources.nlb.gov.sg/infopedia/articles/SIP_1072_2010-03-25.html.

UK puppet[422).

Laws and Customs of War on Land (Hague Convention IV), Article I states that "The Contracting Powers shall issue instructions to their armed land forces which shall conform with the regulations respecting the Laws and Customs of War on Land, annexed to the present Convention"[423). Hague Convention IV and Annex Section I on Belligerents chapter I states that the qualifications of belligerents are[424):

> "Article 1. The laws, rights, and duties of war apply not only to armies but also to Militia and volunteer Corps fulfilling the following conditions:
>
> (1) To be commanded by a person responsible for his subordinates;
>
> (2) To have a fixed distinctive emblem recognizable at a distance;
>
> (3) To carry arms openly; and
>
> (4) To conduct their operations following the laws and customs of war."

In countries where Militia or Volunteer Corps constitute the army or form part of it, they are included under the denomination "army". Article 3 also states that cumulative conditions of (1), (2), (3), (4) give a qualfication of the armed forces of the belligerent. When the conditions are met, Militia or Voluntary Corps who are captured by the enemy, both are entitled to a right to be treated as prisoners of war.[425) What is the prisoner of war? Qualification as belligerents is important to be treated as POW. According to (Hague Convention IV) Annex Section II Art. 4, prisoners of war are those fall under the power of the hostile government, but not of the

422) *Ibid.*
423) Article I of Laws and Customs of War on Land (Hague IV) 1907.
424) Laws and Customs of War on Land (Hague IV).
425) Article 3 of Laws and Customs of War on Land (Hague IV).

individuals or corps who capture them.[426] They must be treated humanely. All their personal belongings, except arms, horses, and military papers, should remain as their property.

Furthermore, according to the convention, spies, and it is the activity described in Article 29 until 31 that stated[427]:

> "A person can only be considered a spy when, acting clandestinely or on false pretense, he obtains or endeavors to obtain information in the zone of operations of a belligerent, to communicate it to the hostile party. Thus, soldiers not wearing a disguise who have penetrated the zone of operations of the hostile army, to obtain information, are not considered spies. Similarly, the following are not considered spies: Soldiers and civilians, carrying out their mission openly, entrusted with the delivery of dispatches intended either for their army or the enemy's army. To this class belong likewise persons sent in balloons to carry dispatches and, generally, of maintaining communications between the different parts of an army or a territory (Article 29), spy has taken in the act shall not be punished without previous trial. (Article 30), A spy who, after rejoining the army to which he belongs, is subsequently captured by the enemy, is treated as a prisoner of war and incurs no responsibility for his previous acts of espionage (Article 31)."

To some, Indonesia's bombing of the McDonald house could be considered as an act of clandestine activity against a foreign nation. But at the same time, the Geneva Conventions 1949, common article 3 of the 1949 Geneva Conventions protects;

> "persons taking no active part in the hostilities, including members

426) Customs of War on Land (Hague IV) Annex to the Convention Regulations Respecting the Laws and Customs of War on Land Section II.

427) *Ibid*, Article 29,30 and 31.